SAVANNAH FOOD

A Delicious HISTORY

STU CARD and
DONALD CARD

AMERICAN PALATE

Published by American Palate
A Division of The History Press
Charleston, SC
www.historypress.net

Cover design by Natasha Walsh

First published 2017

ISBN 9781625858337

Library of Congress Control Number: 2016961485

CONTENTS

ACKNOWLEDGEMENTS

There are many wonderful people who made this book possible. Here are a few.

We would like to first thank our wives, Joanie Card and Nevada Card, for their support and encouragement, without which this book would never have been written.

We would like to thank our parents, Stuart Edward Card and Christine Card, for instilling in us both a passion for food and an adventurous spirit.

Thanks to our baby brother, Chef Gordon Card, for the insight and inspiration.

A special thanks also needs to be given to the incredible tour guides and the rest of our team at Savannah Taste Experience Food Tours. Consistently providing five-star tours several times a day, every day, with professionalism and enthusiasm gave us the confidence and freedom from the daily operations to focus on researching and writing this book. So thank you, Lauren Byram, Brandon Bernard, Lorie "Country" Stokes, Lisa Brumfield, Brenda Upsher, Maria Morgan, Pamela Harding, John Brennan and, of course, Shawndra Russell. We are forever grateful.

INTRODUCTION

Savannah is a storyteller's city. A city for tale-spinners and intent listeners. There are stories dripping from the curling, draping Spanish moss whispering legends as old as the giant sprawling live oaks that shade each of the twenty-two remaining city squares of this otherwise well-preserved masterpiece of a town. Every park bench has overheard elaborate musings of so-and-so and such-and-such from every color and shape of life. Every red brick of its ancient sidewalks has pieced together haunting accounts through the shuffle of every sole passing over it. The impossibly massive container ships blare narratives about far-off lands with every bellow of their enormous horns as they barrel their skyscraper-sized frames down the dark river marking the northern boundary of the city.

But it's the yarns spun from the succulent wild Georgia shrimp and tangy sausage decorating the creamy grits of our very first encounter with such a dish that caught our attention first. Or maybe it was the intoxicatingly sweet chocolate chewies. Perhaps it was the crispy scored flounder. Or maybe the shockingly smooth yet robust crab stew dripping from my overfilled spoon. Who can remember anymore? What counts is that it was spellbinding. It was all-encompassing. We were hooked. We had to have more. We had to know more.

When we first started doing "serious research" (i.e., dining at every family-owned or single-entity restaurant we came across) for setting up our first Savannah Taste Experience food tour (late 2011/early 2012), we were almost dumbfounded by the experience. How have we never tasted this before? Why aren't other restaurants in other cities doing it like this? Why haven't we heard about this before? I mean, it's not like we hadn't been to places or had never explored food before. To the contrary, one of us has traveled the globe (from Russia to South Africa, Italy to Canada, the United Kingdom to China), and the other had dined at some of the best restaurants that Chicago, D.C., New York, San Francisco and L.A. have to offer. And yet here we were, staring at a life-changing bowl of soup in a sleepy southern city of less than 150,000 residents.

Every restaurant was better than the last. Every dish made it more difficult to choose a best. There was always something mind-blowing about a dish or a restaurant. Nevertheless, and more often than not, we had never had any experience with such dishes or had any inkling about the chefs. In fact, the only famous name associated with the food culture in Savannah at the time we began "researching" was Paula Deen, and it had been quite a while since she had been seen in the kitchen of her Historic Downtown restaurant, Lady & Sons.

At first, we were baffled by this phenomenon. There didn't seem to be a chef "celebrity-dom" like so many other cities despite the obvious gastronomic prowess rampant on every corner of its cobbled streets. There were no glossy magazine covers displaying the tattooed arms of the "next big thing" to happen to whatever cuisine. There were no grand openings by Tom Colicchio. There were no Wolfgang Pucks, no Charlie Trotters, no Rick Baylesses.

It felt very much like we were discovering some hidden treasure. Soon, however, our excitement about our culinary expedition was replaced with near debilitating doubt. We began to question our own palates. We even began to worry that we had somehow been drugged by the charm of the city or worse. In all of our collective travels and restaurant experiences throughout the United States, we had never encountered a city with such a concentration of non-chain restaurants producing exceptional yet largely uncelebrated food. On top of that, the restaurant scene was almost completely devoid of household names. So, the issue had to be us. Surely if the cuisine was as good as we thought it was, we would have heard about it or would have noticed the sky beam display of some hot chef's new digs—or at least read a book about the food. Wouldn't we?

Mercifully, our palates were in fine working order. Our confidence in our taste buds was restored when we put down our forks and started chatting with the bartenders, waiters and restaurant owners. Savannahians, as it turns out, are almost militantly polite. It may at times appear as a movie cliché, but certain things are just not discussed among polite folk. One would assume that boasting about the superiority of one's recipe or the uniqueness of one's dish falls into this category. Perhaps it was politeness. Perhaps it was that Charleston had been relishing its own restaurant renaissance since the mid-2000s, drawing a lot of the talent and attention to Savannah's older sister just two hours' drive to the north.

And while times they are a changin' (indeed the dawn of Savannah's culinary revolution is upon us, finally attracting world-class chefs and the recognition the city deserves), up until this point in Savannah's history the food and the food alone told the story. No fuss. No pomp. No flattery. No headlines. Just delicious food.

But given that we are not native Savannahians—having arrived on these shaded streets by choice, not by birth—we hope the city forgives us for helping to share some of the stories of its food and how it arrived at this modern culinary renaissance. As new cutting-edge restaurants open their doors and their ambitious chefs push the bounds of what Savannah cuisine means, it is important to take a moment and digest where it all came from. Having spent the last five years immersed in the culinary scene in Savannah—researching the origins of its fine cuisine—we hope to enlighten its visitors and its new crop of restaurateurs with the fascinating heritage that helps define its modern-day culinary identity.

Chapter 1

THE FAILED EXPERIMENT

S tories of Savannah's favorite dishes are often vague but sometimes lavish and exotic. Mostly, the stories seem to be, well, stories. The chefs, cooks and bakers of these dishes speak of tradition. "This was my grandma's recipe," "this is the way we've always done it" and "this is the way I was taught" are regular responses to inquiries. And while these answers are no doubt true, we were no closer to understanding the origins and details of Savannah's culinary history with such nebulous statements. So, we started where every journey usually commences: the beginning.

Ok, maybe not the *very* beginning, but at least back to the first English written accounts of Savannah as we know it. A very real connection exists between the distinct food of Savannah today and the first days of colonization on its bluff. Savannah's unique history, intensely original characters and varied initial inhabitants planted the seed for its uncommon cuisine of the twenty-first century.

To start with, Savannah—and Georgia, for that matter—began with a set of ideals outrageous at the time. Savannah was not to be a royal colony like the other British colonies—it would serve a higher purpose. The city would be a new start for the insolvent and the indebted, a refuge for the religiously persecuted (such as the Salzburgers) and a land of religious tolerance. Savannah would be a prosperous southern colony without the use of slaves, serving as a shining example of social reform.

This incredible social experiment was the brainchild of English parliamentary member General James Oglethorpe. While many consider

General Oglethorpe a social reformist, there is some cause to question his humanitarian nature. Regardless of his true character, Oglethorpe began the idealistic pursuit of a debtors' colony with a very personal inspiration. In the late 1720s, General Oglethorpe became increasingly disturbed by the overwhelmed debtors' prisons throughout London. His obsession with the debtors' prisons began when his dear friend Robert Castell was imprisoned following debts incurred from publishing a book on architecture. Failure to pay a debt in the 1700s in England, Oglethorpe learned, often resulted in cruel treatment and even starvation in these prisons. Worse yet, debtors' prisons were such widely used resources that not enough prisons existed to house the debtors, forcing many to be imprisoned with quarantined prisoners suffering from a whole host of horrible diseases such as smallpox. That this would be the fate and cause of death of Mr. Castell in 1729 is widely viewed as the catalyst that triggered Oglethorpe's passion for social reform, particularly for the indebted and the poor. Indeed, Oglethorpe began serving on the committee to "Consider a Bill for the Relief of Insolvent Debtors."

A soft spot for the insolvent and the indebted, it turns out, was also a catalyst for the creation of a thirteenth English territory in the Americas. Still incensed by the unnecessary death of Castell, Oglethorpe continued his work regarding insolvent English citizens following the death of Castell. Having just received a £5,000 grant, Oglethorpe enlisted the help of his very influential and powerful friend Lord Percival (later the First Earl of Egmont) to assist in establishing a settlement in the Americas for released debtors.

Oglethorpe knew that another royal colony to the south of the Carolinas (which had only just split into two separate colonies) would not succeed in realizing these ideals. Royal colonies were subject to local governors who were under political and aspirational pressure that would likely jeopardize his lofty goals for the new colony. As such, Oglethorpe, with the assistance of Lord Percival, began organizing support from influential parliamentary members to prepare a proposal that would set up a colony that would allow Oglethorpe, Percival and the other parliamentary members (later to be called the Board of Trustees) to manage and control the colony from England under idealistic tenets to serve others. So different was Oglethorpe's plan for the thirteenth colony of the Americas that those who became trustees were not allowed to own land in the new territory. He even went so far as to establish the motto of the Board of Trustees: *Non sibi sed aliis* ("Not for self, but for others").

A painting of Georgia founder General James Oglethorpe.

By September 1730, a proposal for a new settlement between the Savannah and the Altamaha Rivers—a disputed territory between Spanish Florida and the English colonies of South Carolina at the time—was submitted to Parliament. However, not wanting further conflict with the Spanish, nor finding the benefit in assisting insolvents, Prime Minister Robert Walpole let the proposal lag for more than a year in Parliament's board of trade.

Oglethorpe did not yield in his pursuit for this new territory. Oglethorpe's pressure via Lord Percival and the other influential trustees helped to eventually push the proposal to be reviewed by the Privy Council (the executive body of Parliament). Nevertheless, in the process of trying to establish this debtors' colony, the charitable purpose of the colony gave way to a much broader plan in order to sway the Privy Council. Several revisions were made to the charter proposal in order for it to pass, one of which listed a number of other reasons for the establishment of the Province of Georgia: protecting English interests in South Carolina and helping to relieve English dependence on foreign trade by providing wine, flax, hemp and silk to manufacturers in England. Regardless of these additional interests and influences on the new territory, Oglethorpe eventually got his charter in 1732 and arrived with 114 settlers on February 12, 1733.

Despite the compromises made in establishing the charter, Oglethorpe continued to pursue the idealistic settlement he originally set out to make. He promised free land and assistance with food (Georgia's charter included subsidies from England to help with such promises—the only colony to be supported by subsidies) to the new settlers. This offer was also very different compared to the establishment of the other colonies, which were originally inhabited by those who could afford to make the journey, buy land and slaves and cultivate the land.

That is not to say, however, that General Oglethorpe promised a utopia for those who were to be the first settlers. Before the *Anne* even left the London port, the would-be settlers had to endure an interview and analysis of their worthiness by the trustees themselves. The settlers were also warned that there would be hardship and that they would be expected to work to help develop the new colony. They were also warned from the outset that the weather of the new settlement was intensely hot and humid—not to mention the area was known to have aggressive gnats and mosquitoes.

For those hardy enough to endure the anticipated difficulties, General Oglethorpe insisted on a set of strict provisions that each settler agreed to abide by. These rules were necessary, as Oglethorpe saw it, if his ambitious goals were to succeed. First, hard liquor was banned (although wine and beer were permitted) in an effort to limit disorderliness. Lawyers were also prohibited in Savannah for fear of interfering with or disrupting progress. Further, Roman Catholics were not allowed in the territory for fear of sympathizing with the Spanish settlers still occupying Florida at the time and with whom the English were still engaging in military battles. Jews were also originally prohibited, but this prohibition was lifted almost immediately given the need for doctors (a Jewish doctor having assisted many of the original settlers). These latter two provisions were strangely not seen as contradictions to the ideal of religious tolerance and freedom in the new colony.

The biggest of all of these provisions was the ban on slavery. This was of much concern to the new settlers, having observed the vast wealth their Carolinian counterparts amassed on the backs of their slaves. Oglethorpe was insistent on this ban, however, not for altruistic reasons but rather because he feared his settlers would become lazy. Worried that his critics would prove him wrong (that a settlement of insolvents could become successful and a solution for debtors' prisons), Oglethorpe fought his settlers' 1735 petition to allow slaves. Those who wish to argue that Oglethorpe was not a humanitarian and not as much a social reformist as he touted himself to be point to this issue as evidence, for Oglethorpe did indeed "borrow" slaves from wealthy Charlestonians to clear the land and help build the first of Savannah's buildings. Regardless of Oglethorpe's motives, Georgia was the only colony to prohibit slavery—a prohibition that remained intact during the entirety of Oglethorpe's involvement with the Board of Trustees.

As these initial settlers began to prepare this new outpost on Yamacraw Bluff, on the southern bank of the Savannah River, a second wave of settlers to Savannah was being organized. These settlers would include the Salzburgers—Protestants seeking asylum and refuge following persecution and banishment from their home in what is now Austria at the hands of a Catholic count—and 177 Scottish Highlanders. In 1734, a few of Oglethorpe's trustees were able to secure the support of these Scottish Highlanders under the command of John McIntosh—most of whom hailed from Inverness-shire in the northeast of Scotland and were known for their militaristic fortitude—to be the first guardians of this new settlement.

Both the Salzburgers and the Scots played vital roles in Savannah's history and heritage as time went on, but both established their own towns just outside Savannah. The Salzburgers founded Ebenezer to the west, and the Scots set up New Inverness in what is now known as Darien to the south of the city.

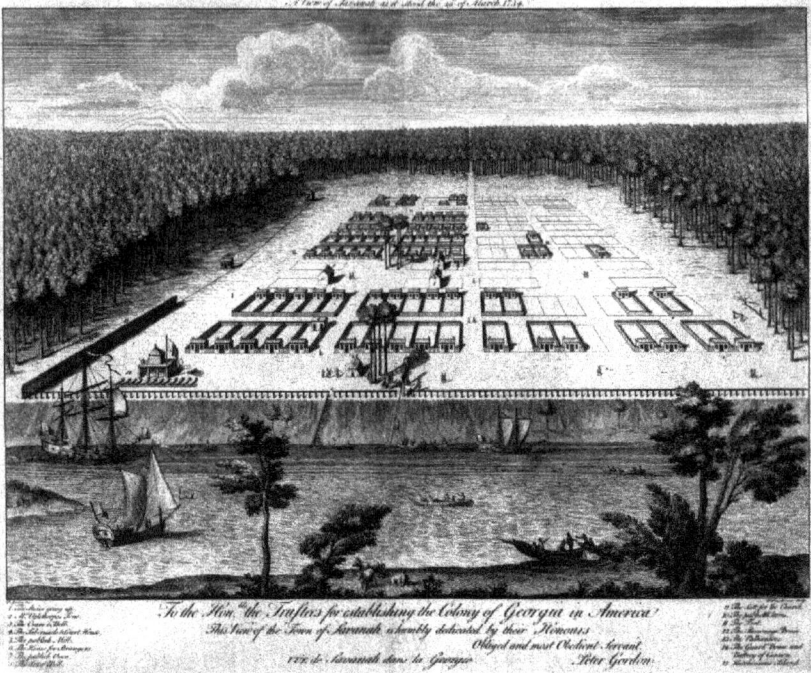

A view of Savannah as it stood in 1734. 1735. *P. Fourdrinier.*

And so Savannah's original western inhabitants were hardy but poor English settlers, Scottish Highlanders and Austrian-German religious refugees. These new Georgians had no farms, little experience growing their own food, few tools and no idea what would grow in the area. As noted earlier, Oglethorpe delivered on his promise to continue to provide sustenance to the settlement but asked in return that an experimental garden be established to discover what crops would best grow in Savannah—hoping not so much to provide for the new inhabitants of the area as to discover a great cash crop to appease his experiment's sponsors.

During this discovery period, as the Trustees' Garden was being developed, most of Savannah's foodstuffs were brought in from Charleston on regular shipments. However, these foodstuffs were not always the same ingredients and products to which these early settlers were accustomed. For example, there were no barley and oats grown such as the Scots would have been accustomed to, and the Salzburgers weren't successful in producing rice in large quantities until the 1750s. Changes to traditional European recipes began to take shape. As the settlers began to experiment with new and often missing ingredients, they, too, began to experiment with the Trustees' Garden.

Great interest was given to the Trustees' Garden in the early days. Primarily, it was the hope of Oglethorpe's sponsors that Georgia would provide silk and wine, so much attention was given to developing mulberry groves to feed the worms that make the silk and noble grapes. While noble grapes were not common in Georgia, local subtropical grape varietals were in abundance. Some pushed for exotic fruit trees, olives and chestnuts, which were in high demand but had to be imported to England. Others pushed for more practical harvests like hops for beer and crops useful in naval rigging like flax and hemp.

Little wine was produced. Chestnut production never worked, and olives were equally unsuccessful at first. Few fruits survived. No useful yields of hemp or flax were produced. Although mulberry and magnolias were successful in the area, silk-making was only measurably successful in Ebenezer (the Salzburgers), where the silk was spun for fishing lines. In fact, the Salzburgers' gardens were the only successful produce production in the early years of Savannah. There are several accounts of Salzburgers selling their produce to the Savannahians, who continued to struggle to produce much on their own. Ebenezer became an invaluable resource for Savannah in these early days, as the resourceful Austrian-Germans continued to thrive in their new home.

Savannahians, who were given land within the city of Savannah as well as grants to purchase up to five hundred acres to establish plantations just outside downtown, continued to struggle in the harsh, hot and humid conditions. Noble Jones, a loyal soldier of Oglethorpe's, was the first to take advantage of this grant, and his is one of the only such plantations still in existence today. The Wormsloe Plantation (named after the Welshman's family's homeland) was one of the few plantations to survive the difficult first twenty-odd years of Georgia's history, but that is not to say that the Wormsloe Plantation was producing a whole lot. To the contrary, the plantation survived the first two dozen years primarily as a military outpost rather than a crop-producing farm. In other words, with Wormsloe as the best example of Oglethorpe's plan, it is clear that the experimental garden and the social experiment in general was struggling to take hold in Georgia.

To make matters worse for the new colony, following several disagreements with the board on the laxation of the rule banning rum in Savannah, along with other disputes, Oglethorpe—the founder and biggest champion of Savannah's potential—attended his last Board of Trustees meeting in

1749. The board tried to continue in Oglethorpe's absence, but the poor performance of the Trustees' Garden and the overall failure of the social experiment overwhelmed the board. In 1751, only nineteen years after its inception, the Board of Trustees relinquished its charter, and King George II converted Georgia to a royal colony. This meant, among other things, that Savannahians were thus legally allowed to acquire slaves, and the plantation system of its northern neighbors was instituted. It didn't take long thereafter for Savannah and Georgia to become major southern cash crop developers.

In the first twenty years as a royal colony, younger Savannahians cultivated a disdain for the overly taxing British government alongside the newly established rice paddies of the Lowcountry. The city nearly tore itself in half as a deep division grew between loyalists and rebels. Incredible secretive divisions grew between mentors and mentees, between sons and fathers.

TONDEE'S TAVERN

The tale of the American Revolution in the South, particularly in Georgia, centers on one restaurant: Tondee's Tavern. Were it not for this simple restaurant, which was at the time on the northwest corner of Broughton and Whitaker Streets in Savannah, it is uncertain the American Revolution would have had much success at all in the South.

But truly, the story begins with two boys at an orphanage. The second-oldest orphanage in America, the Bethesda Home for Boys, was the brainchild of Savannah's charismatic pastor of the Christ Church (the Anglican Church of England in Georgia), George Whitefield. In 1740, following a number of orphaned children, the Bethesda Home for Boys became a necessity. Whitefield, with the help of wealthy donors and the use of the same land grant that Noble Jones used to establish Wormsloe Plantation, bought five hundred acres south east of Savannah abutting Wormsloe.

In the original population of this orphanage was a sixteen-year-old boy who had been floating from family to family with his brother since July 1733, ever since their father died within a few months of arrival in Savannah. Sixteen was quite an old age for a male in his situation in the 1740s, as most boys that age would have been starting an apprenticeship of sorts. Nevertheless, George Whitefield needed free labor (slave labor still being outlawed in Savannah at the time), and the boy, Peter Tondee, needed a place to stay and food to eat. Peter helped construct Bethesda's Great House.

Noticing his propensity for carpentry and hard work, carpenter James Papot soon made Peter Tondee his apprentice.

At the same time, thirteen-year-old Lachlan McIntosh, along with his brother, William, appeared at the orphanage, following the multiple captures and eventual death of their father, John McIntosh, the commander of Oglethorpe's original Scottish Highlanders. Lachlan and William spent two years at the orphanage before Oglethorpe pulled them out to join his military regiment on Fort Frederica on St. Simons Island (about two hours south of Savannah). There Lachlan would learn a great deal of military strategy under Oglethorpe's mentorship.

Oglethorpe's relationship and trust with the McIntoshes had so grown in the three years of his tutelage that he was able to convince the young Scottish Highlanders to abandon their plan to leave Savannah in order to join the Scots' Jacobite Rebellion in 1745. However, after learning that more than 1,500 Scottish Highlanders had been slaughtered in the Battle of Culloden in 1746 (ending the Jacobite uprising), Lachlan was bitterly upset with himself for heeding Oglethorpe's advice in staying out of the conflict, believing that his involvement may have somehow altered the outcome. His disillusionment grew, and as a result, by 1770 McIntosh had become instrumental in the organization of the independence movement in Georgia. Oglethorpe, who was himself influential in the defeat of the Jacobites twenty-five years earlier, was not able to convince his former Scot pupil from engaging so strenuously against British rule in the colonies.

Meanwhile, Peter Tondee had gone on to become a master carpenter, had built and ran his own tavern in Savannah and was the president of the Masonic Lodge in Savannah. Solomon's Lodge No. 1, the first Masonic lodge of Georgia and the "Oldest Continuously Operating English Constituted Lodge of Freemasons in the Western Hemisphere" despite being founded by Freemason Oglethorpe in 1734, had become instrumental in stripping British control of Savannah by 1770.

The then-president of Savannah's Freemasons, Peter Tondee, coordinated efforts with his northern Masonic brothers in Pennsylvania and Massachusetts. Tondee assisted in the orchestration of the gathering of the Liberty Boys (considered a part of Samuel Adams's Sons of Liberty, based out of Massachusetts) in what was known as the Long Room of Tondee's Tavern. With Peter Tondee standing at the door allowing only those on his list to enter, they gathered around a long table, undoubtedly with pints of Savannah's finest ale and a selection of the city's greatest tavern food;

military and diplomatic positions were discussed, plans were detailed and divisions were drawn.

Some of these secretive diners not only are known to us but also illustrate just how sharply a divide there was between the generations of Savannahians. Of note, Noble Wimberly Jones drew the ire of his devout loyalist father, Noble Jones (a proud member of Oglethorpe's Forty-Second Regiment of Foot that fought in the War of Jenkins' Ear), when the younger Jones encouraged the Georgia Commons House in its rejection of the Townshend Act of 1768 and other notable acts of rebellion against the Crown. Jones the elder felt so betrayed by his son that he was written out of the will, causing the beloved and beautiful Wormsloe Plantation to bypass the younger Jones and bequeath instead to Noble Wimberly's younger sister, Mary Jones Bulloch. The elder Jones died in 1775, before the war began.

Three Scotsmen were also known to dine at the Long Room. Lachlan McIntosh, previously discussed, would go on to become a brigadier general of the Continental army. Fighting under McIntosh, Archibald Bulloch would be chosen to be Georgia's first president and commander in chief. Bulloch was born in Charleston, South Carolina, shortly after his parents moved from Scotland. The influence of this particular Tondee's Tavern diner on the history of the United States cannot be understated, for not only was Bulloch influential in the American Revolution itself, but he is also the great-great-grandfather of one the country's most cherished presidents, Theodore Roosevelt. The third of the Scottish Liberty Boys was Edward Telfair. Telfair, a man with only a grammar school education and a Georgia resident since 1766, became the first and a multi-term governor of Georgia, a signer of the Articles of Confederation and one of only twelve men who had electoral votes to be the first president of the United States of America.

On a particularly rambunctious night, shortly after hearing the news of the Battles of Lexington and Concord, thirty young Georgian rebels met at Tondee's Tavern on June 4, 1775—the night of King George III's birthday—and toasted American liberty leaders at each of the thirty cannon fires punctuating the king's age, following which they marched through Savannah with bayonets challenging a confrontation that never came. One month later, the more sober group met as the Second Provincial Congress in the Long Room and began putting together the first government of what would be the State of Georgia.

As the story goes, America gained its independence, and the bloody conflict between Britain and America ended with the Treaty of Paris in

1783. Unfortunately, Peter Tondee died before even the Declaration of Independence was signed. The group continued on at the Liberty Boys' favorite dining establishment without Tondee, and despite losing Savannah to the British in 1778, Tondee's Long Room continued to be utilized as a state planning headquarters. In fact, following the rebels' win at the Battle of Yorktown, the State of Georgia returned to its original headquarters, Tondee's Tavern, while the terms of the treaty were being discussed.

Thus, while little is known of the food served in Tondee's Tavern in the 1770s, there is little doubt that the restaurant is one of the most important dining establishments in all of Georgia. Regrettably, a fire ravaged Savannah in 1796, wiping out the master carpenter's crowning achievement and the birthplace of Georgia as we know it. Today, the lot that once held the most important conversations of this country is once again a place of gathering, enjoying great ales and communing: Coffee Fox, an extraordinary Savannah coffeehouse by Savannah College of Art and Design (SCAD) alum Jennifer Jenkins. Also, in honor of this most important of all Georgian dining institutions, Savannah native Willie Tuten opened a Tondee's Tavern on the corner of Bay and Bull Streets, serving great local cuisine.

THE PIRATES' HOUSE

The very idea of a pirate-themed restaurant may cause some culinary tourists to cringe. But the eatery doesn't use the theme for the sole sake of drawing customers with its gimmick. The truth is that the restaurant is the oldest in Georgia. In the wake of the failed experiment of the Trustees' Garden, which left malnourished soil and rotting plants, there arose a wee inn destined to birth legends as vast as the seven seas. In 1753, a restaurant was born and has remained such ever since.

The name of the restaurant stems from a series of rumors, legends and myths originating in the mid-nineteenth century. While few of these fantastic stories can be verified in any real way, they have so often been repeated and there have been so many various accounts of similar occurrences that there is little reason to doubt the general premise that the restaurant was originally a hot spot for pirates of the eighteenth and nineteenth centuries, who were known to raid boats up and down the southeastern seaboard. One of the most often-repeated stories concerns a young local police officer who stopped by the establishment for a cocktail but instead found himself aboard a large ship headed to China after a few too many. Legend has it

Above: The Pirates' House Restaurant from Broad Street. Circa 1939. *Frances Benjamin Johnston.*

Left: Watkins Famous Restaurants—old recipes of famous restaurants; starred by Pirates' House. *Courtesy of John Nichols.*

that secret tunnels under the rum cellar led out to the end of the bluff on Savannah River, where ships would regularly dock. If captains of such ships were unable to find enough men for the crew, unsuspecting bar patrons were over-served rum or otherwise drugged and dragged out through the tunnels only to wake as an involuntary crew member of a pirate ship. Such was the fate of this unfortunate police officer for whom it took more than two years to return to Savannah, it is said.

The legendary pirate status of this eatery was cemented when prominent nineteenth-century Scottish author Robert Louis Stevenson reportedly utilized some of the fantastic stories about the tunnels he'd heard while staying at this inn in writing his classic *Kidnapped*. Further adding to the mystique of this restaurant, Stevenson is also said to have based the backstory of Captain Flint of another of his classic tales, *Treasure Island*, on characters he encountered at this restaurant. Indeed, Stevenson even wrote that Captain Flint died in Savannah shouting, "Fetch aft the rum."

The restaurant has, of course, changed hands over the past 260-plus years. Additions have been made, and preservation efforts have been managed. The restaurant is now a series of old buildings connected together in a near labyrinth of ancient wood and brick. One of the restaurant's dining areas is the first floor of the oldest building in Georgia, the Herb House, which was the home of the Trustees' Garden's gardener. The Herb House was erected in 1734. What we consider the Pirates' House today really began in 1948, when the wife of the president of Savannah Gas Company began reworking the buildings into the restaurant we now know. Having changed hands since 1948, the spot continues to thrive as both a restaurant and a living museum of a strange part of Savannah's history.

The current menu features a host of southern fare one would expect to find south of the Mason-Dixon line. One dish that does stand out as a unique spin on a southern favorite is the restaurant's Honey Pecan Fried Chicken. This is a perfect marriage of sweet, savory, crunchy, crispy and tender. And with Georgia producing more pecans than anywhere else in the world, it is a fitting addition to the traditional southern dish.

Olde Pink House

It's fair to say that visitors and locals alike would visit James Habersham Jr.'s lovely mansion whether they were serving great food inside or not—it's beautiful, it has a ton of history and it is one of the only great buildings in Savannah still standing after the 1796 fire wiped out half of the city (the very same fire that wiped out the original Tondee's Tavern). It would be toured as often as guests tour famed nineteenth-century architect William Jay's regency-style masterpiece, the Owens-Thomas House, on Oglethorpe Square in Savannah. Many history buffs would undoubtedly marvel at the artifacts of this great home as at John Norris's Gothic Revival Green-Meldrim House, where Union general Sherman set up his headquarters for the last year of the Civil War. But add white linens, fine dining service and crispy scored flounder and you have a unique recipe that has long been a staple food stop in Savannah.

The house had a long road to becoming one of Savannah's busiest restaurants. In fact, it had a long road to becoming a house at all. James Habersham Jr., wealthy cotton factor (a merchant who sold and traded cotton but did not necessarily grow it himself) and son of the original administrator over the Bethesda Orphanage project, broke ground on the building in 1771 but would not complete the home for another eighteen years. One of the biggest delays in the completion of the house came during the Revolutionary War, leading up to the failed Siege of

The Habersham House in 1933, what is now known as the "Olde Pink House." Circa 1933. *Historic American Buildings Survey.*

Savannah in 1779—an incredibly bloody and protracted battle that cost the revolutionaries more than eight hundred men, including celebrated freedom fighters Count Casimir Pulaski and Sargent William Jasper—when British forces occupied the home. This was a particularly insulting occurrence for James Habersham Jr., as he did not exactly share his father's loyalist ideals. James Jr. was more aligned with his brother's perspective, Joseph Habersham being one of the known Liberty Boys.

Regardless, James Jr. was lucky enough to regain control of his home in 1783 with the signing of the Treaty of Paris. Over the next several years, James continued to struggle to build the pristine white colonial mansion of his dreams. The most vexing of Habersham's building woes came in the plastering of the red brick house. Despite multiple efforts, the red brick base bled through the white plaster, giving the house a pink hue. Habersham finally resigned himself to the idea that he would simply have to repaint his house white on a regular basis. The color of the house may not have been of the quality that Habersham had wished, but the structure of the building was sound. The house bore witness to a fire in 1796, wiping out half of the city's buildings, as well as a fire in 1820, without damage.

Following Habersham's death, the house was used and abused by a number of different institutions. Two different banks occupied the house for about fifty years, until 1865, when Union general Zebulon York used the house as his headquarters. The first instance of the house being used for the service industry was in 1920, when Alida Harper turned the prestigious property into a teahouse. Harper was the first of the home's owners to not paint the house white and just allow the pink hue of the plaster to become the signature of the building that it was always meant to be.

Finally, after years of neglect, the house was bought by Charleston's Balish family (who had successful restaurants in Charleston and Columbia, such as Garibaldi's in Five Points; the family now also owns Garibaldi's restaurant in Savannah) in 1992 with the intention of turning it into a restaurant. The plan was to restore the building to its former eighteenth-century glory, and that meant hiring one man: Jim Williams. The Habersham House is one of several houses Williams has restored in Savannah, contributing to his vast wealth gained mostly through antiques dealing as well as restoring Savannah homes. And while Williams's contributions to Savannah home restoration include both the exquisite work that he did himself as well as contributing several important essays on home preservation, it was the legendary parties at his own renovated home, the Mercer House (originally built for Johnny Mercer's great-grandfather General Hugh Weedon Mercer), for which he was most well known in the city. That is, until Jim Williams shot his lover to death in the Mercer House study, setting off a chain of events immortalized in John Berendt's 1994 bestseller *Midnight in the Garden of Good and Evil*.

By the time "the book" (as it is known in Savannah) flew off the shelves to become a national bestseller, and certainly by the time Clint Eastwood turned the book into a movie, the Habersham House was known only as the Olde Pink House Restaurant. Crispy scored flounder is a signature dish for the restaurant and a delight for the senses. Apricot and shallot sauce set just enough sweetness to balance out the plate.

The restaurant is known as one of the busiest in Savannah and has been for some time. Is it the fact that the house dates back to Savannah's colonial era that keeps this restaurant so busy? Or is it the mystique of dining in a Jim Williams–renovated eighteenth-century Georgian mansion? Or perhaps is it the great, locally inspired dishes? Yes to all, we'd say.

Chapter 2

FINDING THE RIGHT INGREDIENTS

An important part of the quest to find Savannah's culinary identity really began at the almost surreal Zunzi's TakeOut on the corner of York and Drayton Streets—an award-winning sandwich counter that infuses South African flavors with Roma-Italian traditions and techniques. Zunzi's is one of those special places that is hard to come by in most cities, a place that doesn't exactly make sense in its surroundings but could only really happen right where it is. It is simultaneously a product of its local environment and of the world. At any rate, there is little doubt anyone who has ever tasted the original but somehow familiar and comforting food from its counter has become addicted.

It is a "counter" because while there may be a few outdoor tables around the corner, slightly cordoned off from the parking lot where they stand, the door to Zunzi's merely opens to a counter with enough width for one normal human to fit. A literal hole-in-the-wall restaurant. Savannah College of Art and Design (SCAD) students, lawyers, firefighters and tourists alike will line up against the brick wall every day of the week (save for Sundays, when it is generally closed) in the baking sun to get their fix of Conquistador or Godfather sandwiches—the former an en papillote chopped-chicken sandwich and the latter the same but with a choice of either smoked or South African sausage.

The tangy, earthy South African sausage on the Godfather sandwich triggers contemplation. This is not an ordinary sausage, and the staff at Zunzi's admit that it is an acquired taste (hence the option of a more

A view of the old farmers' market. *Courtesy of John Nichols.*

American palate–friendly smoked sausage). The South African variety of sausage is such a unique taste that it begs the question as to how one would come by such a taste in Savannah. Is there a South African butcher somewhere in the area? Is there a secret South African sausage-making society in Savannah?

It turns out that Zunzi's originally made its own sausage. However, the time-consuming process became more costly in the small kitchen compared to having it outsourced. The only butcher the owners trusted with this process was Savannah's very own Smith Brothers Butcher Shop.

Smith Brothers Butcher Shop settled on the quiet east side of Liberty Street when the fabled meat shop and market returned to the Historic Downtown in 2015. Zunzi's sausages aside, stories abound of a few cattle farming brothers who in the 1920s sold their select cuts out of a stall in the City Market. While the brothers have long passed, the rumors were that the traditions of south Georgian cattle and pig farming were still honored in the butcher shop where they originated in 1924, a butcher shop that meticulously curates its beef, pork and produce from select local farmers.

The beautifully understated building that is now the home of this butchery is quintessential Savannah. Its only subtle decoration are a few worn, carefully placed horizontal barn timbers under the raised logo of the shop. It looks modern with its otherwise sharp white exterior walls, but it somehow seems like it has always been there. It is incredibly inviting.

After swinging the large glass doors open, we were met with a feast for the eyes and nose. To our left, a dizzying array of local fresh produce. Our eyes followed the rows of local vegetables, legumes and herbs until they eventually gave way to a deli counter and cheese display at the far end of the store. To our right, running the length of the store, was a very healthy selection of wines capable of complementing any dish that could be devised from the incredible ingredients available throughout the space. But it was center of the store that consumed most of our attention. Display cases of various dry-aged beefs—some cut to show off the expertise of the butcher and others left for the consumer's request—shone bright and crisply clear like a homing beacon. This was a clear and purposeful message: meat is at the center of this business. Behind the meat display case was a set of large windows behind which three men busily maneuvered in their enclosed cutting room preparing some lucky soul's New York strips, rib-eye, pork chops or some other glorious meat dish.

There is clearly more than just the answers to the origins of Zunzi's South African sausage here. A closer look reveals that many of the culinary roads in Savannah go through Smith Brothers. As one would expect from native Savannahians, Smith Brothers' current owners, Robert and Brenda Anderson, would be too polite to admit to it.

Robert could not make butchery and small market ownership look more refined. He is always dapper. His apron for walking the front of the house has thick navy stripes and is without a stain. His snow-white and

Smith Brothers Butcher Shop, Liberty Street, Savannah, Georgia. 2016. *Donald Card.*

bushy, immaculately maintained goatee can't hide his smile and his love for what he does. His look and demeanor is quite honestly timeless. He is the opposite of a fad—he is the physical incarnation of what a shop owner used to be and should always be.

Robert Anderson has been butchering in Savannah since he was thirteen years old and working in his father's market. On the day of his birth, Robert's mother rushed out of Savannah to Reidsville, Georgia (about forty-five minutes west of Savannah), to deliver her son in the hospital where her sister worked, so he blushes at the suggestion that he was "born and raised" in Savannah. Nonetheless, his knowledge of Savannah's way of life before the tourism rush of the late 1990s and into present day is evident in the proud and dignified manner in which he conducts himself and his business.

There are shortcuts that one could take in running a small local downtown market. Of course it would be cheaper to buy meats and produce from large corporate-owned farms and their distributors. Of course it is more convenient (and perhaps even cheaper) for a modern shopper to buy cheap, frozen meats, cheeses and produce in bulk from large chain grocery stores. But that doesn't mean that is the way it should be. Robert and his wife, Brenda, know better and, without lecturing anyone, show the city how much better life was and can be when you buy fresh, locally sourced foods from people who know about the foods they sell and how those foods are grown. It's so much more than that. The Andersons know exactly what the reasons are for carrying what is in their store at any given time. And so does their staff—a few of whom have lovingly devoted their entire professional life to the market. They know the growers. They work with the growers and slaughterers to be sure to promote what is in season and what will be good next week so that they avoid wastage. They engage their growers to help make sure their growers can sustain themselves. They make sure they are selling the best beef, pork, chicken and produce that Savannah can get.

These are no doubt lessons that Robert learned, and learned well, from his father, Robert ("Andy") Anderson Sr. Andy began his career as a salesman of sorts for small local grocery stores such as Food Town. He went on to learn as much of the small market business as he could, including learning how to butcher meat. Armed with enough knowledge and proverbial vinegar, Andy opened his own small (only a few hundred square feet by some accounts) market called "Andy's" in 1973. In the early years of the store, Andy would spend his days working for Barney Sadler, owner of Food Town, and his nights cutting meats in his own store. As the store became more successful, Andy enlisted the help of his then thirteen-year-old son, Robert. Robert began cutting chickens and simple meat cuts. By the time Robert had made it through his teen years, he was well versed in the small market and butchery business.

Andy's butchers and market continued to grow, and Robert happily helped see his father's business expand to three locations throughout the Savannah area. It was therefore no surprise that Robert would continue on in his father's business when it was time for Andy to step back. But it was Robert's steadfast desire to run the butchers and markets in a traditional sense and not give way to fads or attempts to make quick bucks that landed Robert at the helm of his competitor (Smith Brothers Butcher Shop) in 1993.

Smith Brothers Butcher shop today is, as previously noted, as modern as it is timeless. As much as Robert and Brenda have honored the Smith Brothers' legacy, they have also, either consciously or subconsciously, imprinted the store, its foodstuffs and its operations with quintessential Anderson flair. Robert and Brenda were sure to maintain the staff of Smith Brothers—a few of whom are still proudly on the payroll today, just as they have been since the mid-1960s. However, as much as the Andersons tried to hold on to Smith Brothers' traditions, many things had changed since the first time Leon and Harry Smith sold their first cut of meat in the old City Market.

The days have long gone when the brothers Smith slaughtered their cattle, butchered the meat and hauled the goods to be sold out of a small stall at the old City Market at what is now Ellis Square. To be fair, the days are also long gone when the City Market functioned as a traditional market of local produce, meats and fishes. Today, the City Market is a bustling tourist center (just west of Ellis Square now) with local art studios, souvenir shops and restaurants.

Nevertheless, for the first several years of the Smith Brothers enterprise, Leon and Harry were the farmers, the slaughterers, the butchers, the distributers and the merchants. As the reputation of Smith Brothers meats grew, it became necessary to hire a variety of staff and have a more permanent storefront location near downtown Savannah. Sometime prior to 1966, Leon and Harry stopped the slaughtering operations, as it proved more cost effective to outsource that task, despite maintaining the sixty-plus acre farm in Hagan, Georgia (about a forty-five-minute drive west of downtown).

By September 1966, George Thomas, then the son-in-law of Leon Smith, was in charge of the family's farm and butchers. Mr. Thomas—a chemist by training—managed both entities, but analysis of the business pushed him to lease several acres of the farm to other farmers, and eventually Leon and Harry's farm stopped supplying the butchers altogether, again finding it made more business sense to buy its meat supply from other local farmers. Mr. Thomas would still use the remaining portions of the farm for butcher store staff picnics and hunting.

As the winds of change may have begun for the Smith Brothers Butcher shop in the 1960s and '70s, so, too, were they changing for the entire city of Savannah. Brenda McDougald and her high school sweetheart, Robert Anderson, enjoyed the rhythm of Savannah in those years but saw the necessity for change. Miss McDougald (who would soon be Mrs. Anderson) is blissful in her recounting of strolls with her butcher beau down the cobblestone road of River Street (actually composed of the ballast stones that kept the cotton ships from capsizing on their journey from England and then unloaded on Savannah's shore to make room for bales of cotton, long before there were hotels, souvenir shops or restaurants). By some accounts, there were really only three restaurants on or near River Street worth visiting in those days—Boar's Head Grill, Peddlers and Hesters Martinique (of these only Boar's Head Grill remains; more on that later)— and River Street was not a place Father McDougald was happy seeing his daughter spending any length of time given the boarded-up buildings, dark alleys and constant reports of criminal activity up and down the one-mile stretch of river frontage.

Indeed, many accounts of River Street prior to the 1980s were that of a skid row type. Where now are gift shops were once boarded-up, dilapidated old cotton warehouses. The cobblestone where the one-track trolley now occasionally runs, to the delight of the tourists, used to drop off into the mud and marsh of the riverbank. Many of the ancient steps down from the top of the thirty-foot bluff where the rest of Savannah sits had not yet been fitted with modern handrails. It wasn't until 1979, when Mayor John Rousakis began his urban renewal project on River Street and throughout the Historic District, that there was anything that resembled a river walk. It was thus not until the 1980s and '90s that Savannah's now famous River Street had any shops or restaurants beyond Boar's Head Grill.

Although the city may not have been the thriving tourist destination that it is today, Brenda and Robert continued to enjoy their hometown

Dilapidated River Street warehouses before the urban renewal project brought them back to life. Circa 1939–44. *Frances Benjamin Johnston.*

throughout the '60s and '70s. And while major chain stores and restaurants had not yet invaded the shady streets of their beloved city, the two young lovers still had great food, albeit limited in variety. Prior to the litany of choices that Savannah visitors see today, if you wanted meat before 1980, you most likely went to Smith Brothers; for baked goods, you went to Gottlieb's Bakery; and if you wanted any type of local catch, you went to Russo's Seafood. Luckily, these purveyors were both highly skilled and thoughtful about their products, so much so that they are still delighting Savannahians to this day; they are not so obviously found to the casual tourist, though, as none of these great Savannah staples has an awning on River Street or City Market. If one wished to seek out the Savannah of yesteryear, one need only ask a Savannahian with at least a thirty-year vintage, someone who remembers when Ellis Square was demolished to make way for a parking garage (and then eventually reverted back to a square) or when Broughton Street's shopping was made up of Kress, JCPenney's and five and dimes. One must look to a time before the talents of Chef Mashama Bailey (The Grey), Chef Hugh Acheson (The Florence) or even Chef Elizabeth Terry (Elizabeth on 37th) were part of the culinary landscape.

By the time River Street had a proper river walk, Brenda McDougald had become Brenda Anderson. In the late '70s and early '80s, Brenda Anderson spent most of her professional time working in the still small hotel industry. In this capacity, Brenda was, in a very real way, a part of the trend to bring visitors to her beloved city. Much attention was spent in trying to come up with ways to encourage visitors to come to Savannah in months other than March/April and September/October. The new restaurants and stores popping up along River Street and the newly updated City Market were asked to assist in promotions, discounts and activities to promote tourism to a city that had never really been a tourist destination. As Brenda explained it, efforts not far from begging were utilized to encourage these new restaurants and shops to design their business models around attracting visitors.

But when Brenda was not working in Savannah's infant hospitality industry, she was assisting her husband in running Andy's markets (later called Andy's IGA). Andy's markets were doing quite well, despite the presence of the long-standing Savannah staple and Andy's competitor, Smith Brothers Butcher Shop.

While certainly Andy's market and Smith Brothers Butcher Shop were competitors in a technical sense, there appears to have been as much a mutual respect between the two main butchers in the Savannah area. Indeed, when George Thomas (owner of Smith Brothers since 1966) decided to sell Smith Brothers Butcher Shop, it is rumored that he made just one call. Robert was more than happy and honored to carry the heritage of the shop forward. In fact, Robert maintained both his father's Andy's and the Smith Brothers brands simultaneously until circumstances led Robert to start closing a few of the shops. He maintained the Smith Brothers brand until all that was left was the Smith Brothers Butcher Shop on Skidaway Island. Moreover, when Robert and Brenda decided to take a chance at returning their butcher shop to downtown Savannah in 2015, it was the Smith Brothers brand that Robert chose to maintain due to its history and ties to the city being just a generation longer than his own family's. (As a happy side note, the land previously used for the cattle of the Smith Brothers Butcher Shop is still held by the descendants of Harry and Leon Smith.)

In its downtown Savannah location, the center display case holds precut rib-eyes with beautiful marbling, bone-in New York strips and a few roast cuts. Smith Brothers Butcher Shop dry-ages certain cuts of beef an additional thirty to forty-five days beyond the already thirty days' worth of dry-aging the primal cuts have already gone through before they arrive at the store. This additional aging ensures that Smith Brothers' steak has the best flavor and is the most tender of any other steak in Savannah. This additional dry-aging further assists the evaporation of moisture in the meat and allows oxygen to aid the lactic acid in naturally breaking down the connective tissue in the muscle. At one time, the entire dry-aging process (both primal cuts and more refined cuts) occurred inside the butchers for Smith Brothers, but due to the expense and sheer real estate needed, the first twenty to thirty days of dry-aging is done elsewhere.

This much patience and expense in dry-aging beef in the manner that the Smiths would have done nearly one hundred years ago produces steaks so good and so tender that several restaurants and chefs in the city, like the award-winning Chef Mashama Bailey of The Grey, make frequent visits to Smith Brothers to supply their restaurants with meats and seasonal inspiration. Reportedly, several other restaurants in the Savannah area—even some large high-end chain restaurants—regularly rely on Smith Brothers to delight their customers (or do so upon depletion of the corporate stock).

Around the side of the front-facing display case is another large display case filled almost entirely with sausages, a variety seldom seen in any other butcher shop. There are traditionally seasoned, mixed sausages such as bratwurst, andouille, sweet and hot Italian and smoked sausages. Those slowly give way to more exotic and proprietary sausage blends, such as Smith Brothers' best-selling Tuscan Sausage. There are sausages that could be linked to Germany, Italy, France, South America and

South Africa. And then there are the game changers, like the blueberry breakfast sausages. Yes, you read that correctly: blueberry sausage. And it turns out it is incredible.

The variety and enormous quantity of sausages on display in this large display case begs the question: Why are there so many varieties of sausages in the most respected butchers in Savannah? Has this always been the case? If so, why? And why hasn't Savannah's culinary scene been associated with sausage before? While Robert confesses that he is no historian, he can assure us that Smith Brothers and Andy's have always provided their customers with sausages for a variety of dishes common in the Lowcountry. Sure enough, a quick survey of some of the area's most common dishes—Savannah red rice, shrimp and grits, Lowcountry boils, even biscuits and gravy—often feature some type of sausage. Further, as is the case with most butchers, Smith Brothers is careful not to waste. As such, mirroring that ancient practice of butchers not just in Savannah but throughout Europe, Smith Brothers encourages its meat department to devise interesting and tasty ways to mix butchered scraps and other less popular portions of beef and/or pork with salt, spices and other natural ingredients to create sausage.

In fact, sausage has been a key staple product in Savannah cuisine since the days of the original European inhabitants. The English, the Scottish Highlanders and the Protestant Salzburg refugees all hailed from parts of Europe that depended on these cheaper meat products for sustenance. The cuisines of all three of the original settling cultures had sausage as a significant part.

The Salzburgers, with their Austrian-German heritage, would have certainly been accustomed to bratwurst. Bratwurst had been invented by at least 1432 (records from this year illustrate strict recipes for the sausage) and, by the eighteenth century, was prevalent, with numerous varieties throughout what was then the Holy Roman Empire in Germany. The Salzburgers would have also been exposed to Slovenian sausages (such as Carniolan sausages, which eventually morphed into modern-day kielbasa) given its proximity to the country.

Similarly, a small group of Protestant Germans (actually hailing from an area in what is now the Czech Republic) known as the Moravians arrived in Savannah in 1735, bringing with them their Bohemian sausage traditions. However, the group was rather small (only about forty parishioners in total), and they only stayed in Savannah for about ten years. The Moravians were hoping to expand their wee settlement with the inclusion of about two hundred religiously persecuted refugees from Poland, only to have those refugees decide to settle in Pennsylvania instead. Conflicts also arose between the Moravians and the Salzburgers, and despite his best efforts, John Wesley (then curate of the Christ Church, Savannah's Anglican Church of England, and who would later help to create the Methodist Church) was not able to successfully mediate a resolution between the groups. Nonetheless, there is evidence that Germanic and Bohemian butchering styles and sausage flavors were present in the earliest days of the city.

The Scots also heavily favored their pudding—a British term believed to be the result of anglicizing the French word for sausage, *boudin*. The folklore of haggis suggests that early shepherds' wives would construct a version of what we would consider haggis as a way to ration their food on their long journey to the markets or perhaps even just a way to preserve the otherwise quickly perishable offal (heart, lung, liver) after a hunt. Whatever its origins in Scotland, it has been described in poems and literature as early as 1508 (See "Flyting of Dumbar and Kennedy"—"flyting" being a genre of poetry whereby two poets have a literary battle). Equally as difficult to nail down the origins of, but equally as much a part of Scottish cuisine as the haggis, black pudding (blood sausage) has been part of the Scottish culinary landscape for centuries. In fact, blood sausage is mentioned in some of the oldest known literature. There are references to similar sausages in Homer's *Odyssey* and throughout ancient Roman texts. And although the Scots would have continued to preserve non-choice cuts of animals in sausage, the lack of oats and/or barley in Savannah—a common additive of many Scottish sausages (such as black pudding, haggis, white pudding and so on)—would have changed the form of those sausages substantially.

Similarly, the English had their litany of sausages enjoyed with regional varieties as old as the British kingdom itself. While bangers and mash is of much more recent history, there is no doubt a long history of sausage in English cuisine. From Cumberland to Lincolnshire and the sausages of the Black Country in Northern England, evidence abounds that in Oglethorpe's settling, English debtors would have enjoyed sausages as a staple of their diet.

The sausage-making heritage of Savannah's founders still courses through the veins of today's lively citizens. And locals simply get their sausage from Smith Brothers Butcher Shop and have since the 1920s. One could even hear local radio legend Burl Womack sizzle fresh Smith

Brothers sausage on his morning radio show for more than thirty years. The deep-voiced radio personality was well loved, as evidenced by his legions of followers of his hit show, *Breakfast with Burl*, which aired in the Savannah listening market from 1957 to 1989.

All that having been said, there is no one sausage that Savannah is known for, either in the past or present day, but Savannahians have no doubt always used sausages in various dishes throughout its history. While there is no distinct "Savannah sausage," Robert makes a strong argument for a few of them. The strongest for a trademark Savannah sausage would be the blueberry sausage; with blueberries being in season in Savannah from mid-April through the end of July, there is something refreshing about that sausage to start a very steamy day.

One thing clear about the sausage of Smith Brothers is that it tends to be noticeably coarser than sausages from up north or even Cajun sausages of Louisiana. This is Robert's signature. Robert even convinced Zunzi's to change its secret family's South African sausage recipe to use a coarser grind to the meat. With so many Savannahians having gotten their sausages from Robert (either through Andy's markets or Smith Brothers Butcher Shop) over the years, would it be such a stretch to call this variety of sausage "Savannah style"?

Robert and Brenda finished our tour of Smith Brothers by exploring the mind-boggling selection of cheeses, both local and international; the range of unique Georgian food products such as Thomasville fruit ketchups; the beautiful array of local produce from as close as thirteen miles away; and even a few rows of Georgian craft beers (Southbound Brewing Company and Service Brewing Company, the two main Savannah breweries prominently displayed). We spent quite a lot of time going through the fresh produce and discussing seasonality to some degree. Brenda's eyes lit up with excitement as she explained to us her efforts to work out what seems almost like a consignment deal with farmers to help them sell their cover crop, rather than simply destroying the product once it has done its job of fertilizing the fields. We will revisit this incredible subject at greater length in a few chapters, but nevertheless, we point out now that it is not just the ingredients of beef and pork that are so carefully attended to at Smith Brothers Butcher Shop.

Smith Brothers Butcher Shop and the Andersons leave a lasting impression on anyone fortunate enough to walk through their doors. So much of Savannah's culinary history—by way of restaurants and home kitchens alike—runs through this perfect local grocer. So much of

Savannah's future culinary scene will, too. The storefront provides a peek into the life of Savannahians before the first large chain grocery store planted itself in suburban neighborhoods. Savannah is profoundly lucky to still have a place where shoppers can purchase the food that the soil under their feet produced. Shopping in this store, one could just about have three squares a day enjoying dishes with absolutely no ingredient cultivated from farther than seventy-five miles away. In a world of corporate farming and massive franchised grocery chains, that is quite a feat.

Chapter 3
A SEAFOOD DIET

B eing 20 miles from the Atlantic Ocean and with close to 6 square miles of water making up the 108-square-mile city limits, seafood has always been the most important staple of Savannah's diet. The city and surrounding communities have always teemed with thriving seafood restaurants. Residents still entertain their guests with oyster roasts, Lowcountry boils and shrimp dinners. Savannah is no doubt a seafood town.

However, with so many restaurants dedicated to fish in the city, it can sometimes be hard to find authentic Savannah cuisine and authentic local seafood varieties. On the city's bustling River Street, the most touristy part of the Hostess City, dozens of seafood restaurants have made homes in the old cotton warehouses. Many restaurants receive their seafood frozen and ready to drop in a fryer. This is, of course, not the Savannah way. And although it can be somewhat difficult to get local seafood fresh off the boat due to federal regulations, seafood in this Lowcountry city is still king, and there are still great restaurants and vendors serving up classic dishes with surprising histories in the area.

RUSSO'S SEAFOOD

It's still there. In many ways, it's a miracle it's still there. It began with a family rivalry. Years of secret fish deliveries followed. Near bankruptcy due

"The City and Harbor of Savannah, Georgia," a wood engraving drawn by J.O. Davidson. Circa 1883. Published by *Harper's Weekly*, November 1883.

to a brother's debt all but destroyed the business. Zoning challenges from the neighborhood also occurred. As if there weren't enough challenges, the Georgia Department of Natural Resources (DNR) and federal agencies then began shutting down or drastically limiting commercial fishing in many of the local rivers and the Atlantic, cutting off local supplies of fish, roe and crab. And yet, somehow, Russo's Seafood is still there very much in the same way it was there in 1946.

Russo's Seafood, a family owned and run seafood market, is still running strong with its steely blue-eyed captain at the helm. Savannah—with its vast waterways, marshes, estuaries and access to the Atlantic Ocean—has always been a seafood town, and Charlie Russo's family has been successfully providing Savannahians with their seafood for more than one hundred years. There has always been a demand here for wild Georgia shrimp for Lowcountry boils and shrimp and grits, as well as blue crab for crab stews, oysters for oyster roasts, whiting for fried fish and shad. Nonetheless, the survival of this small seafood market has required Charlie Russo Jr. and his predecessor, Charlie Sr., to adapt and fight.

Charlie Jr. is incredibly proud of the market his daddy built in the 1970s. At an exceedingly sprightly seventy-three years young, Charlie is still very

No longer open, this is a view of A.C. Mathews Seafood Market on what is now Martin Luther King Jr. Boulevard. Circa 1950s. *Courtesy of Charlie Russo.*

passionate about the work that he has been doing more or less for sixty-seven years. Even before starting to help his father clean, scale and gut fish at six years old, Charlie claims rather matter-of-factly that the fish market is and always has been in his blood. He very well may be right. Two generations before his birth, Charlie's maternal grandfather, A.C. Mathews (born Antoni Mateo Canorela), immigrated to Savannah as a teenager from Italy, where he and his brothers, Louis (Charlie's godfather) and Frank Mathews, began a small stand in the old City Market in the early 1900s.

The Mathews boys worked hard to gather what fish they could from the boats docking on what is now River Street to haul up to the old City Market a few blocks away. At first, the brothers diversified their offerings with game birds, but as the demand for seafood grew, seafood became the only product the Mathewses provided. Soon, much of the seafood market in the city was cornered by the family. There was A.C. Mathews Seafood on what is now Martin Luther King Jr. Boulevard, Louis C. Mathews Seafood farther south (also on MLK) and Frank C. Mathews just off Ellis Square on Congress and Barnard Streets.

Little did the Mathewses realize that A.C.'s daughter, Antoinette, would marry the man who would become the Mathewses' greatest competition. Charlie Russo Sr. began learning the fish trade working with Louis Rayola in his Fish Market on Bull Street. Charlie Sr. quickly learned the ropes and rose to a general manager. Unfortunately, due to the ongoing effects of the Great Depression, Charlie traded the fish market for the benefits of working in the U.S. Post Office. However, Charlie never worked at the post office long enough to enjoy any of those benefits, as the Second World War broke out shortly after he began. As did many men during that period, Charlie joined the military and spent most of the war overseas.

The deep effect of World War II was evident on Charlie, who saw life as too short to not enjoy one's work. Thus, instead of returning to the safety and security of the post office, he opened Russo's Seafood in 1946. Opening a competing fish market to his father-in-law, A.C. Mathews, was not exactly received well, and the family rivalry began. A.C. Mathews was so affronted by his son-in-law's new market on Thirty-First Street and Waters Lane that he even went so far as to threaten boycotting certain distributors if they sold any fish to Charlie. From the outset, it seemed that Charlie had to rely on his resourcefulness for survival in the industry his father-in-law dominated, as he began setting up secret deals with the distributors. It is reported that these deals required the distributors to drop off the Russo's load at the DeSoto Truck Stop on the outskirts of town so that A.C. would not learn of the off-the-books deals between the distributors and his son-in-law.

Charlie Sr. also saw the opportunity to rise as the premier fish market in Savannah by modernizing the market practices. He started by designing his fish market from the ground up rather than trying to retrofit a market into an existing space that would likely be more than one hundred years

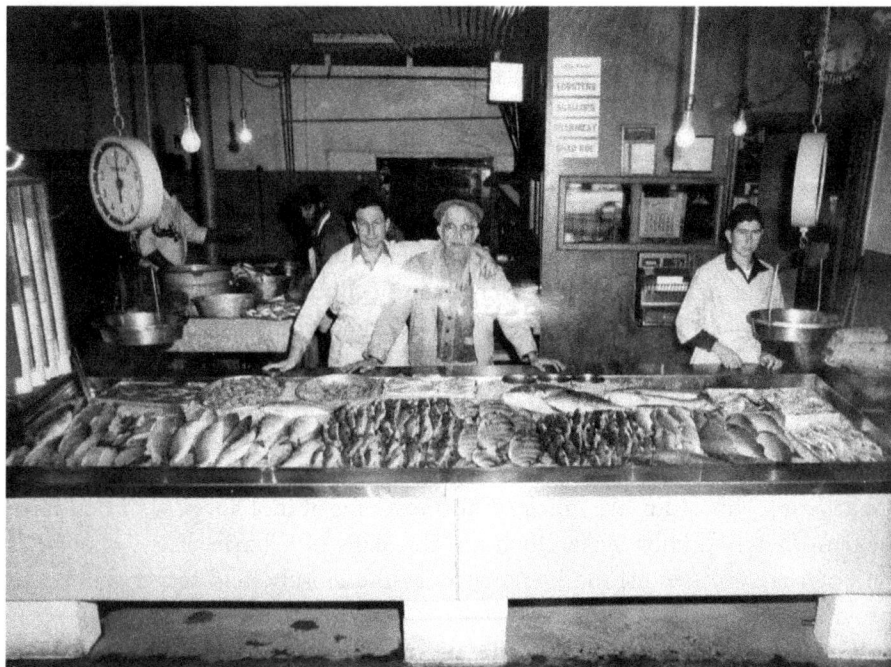

Dedi Mathews, with his arm around Charlie J. Russo Sr. Circa 1950s. *Charlie J. Russo's Seafood.*

old. Charlie met with architects to design a space that would help improve sanitization, allow for custom preparations of the fish in a relatively short time and otherwise improve the efficiency of the market. Even simple things like moving from wrapping the fish and seafood in newspapers, as was the customary practice of his father-in-law and the industry as a whole, to using fresh, clean parchment paper was such a vast improvement in the shopping experience that Russo's soon became the preferred fish market in Savannah. Russo's modernization of the fish market was so revolutionary that the shop became the subject of a book long before legislation and health departments began requiring such practices to be implemented for the health of the general public.

This, however, does not mean that success came easy for Charlie Sr. To the contrary, after lending his truck-driving brother his credit card, his brother then proceeded to rack up approximately $5,000 (an equivalent of about $50,000 in today's money, according to the inflation rates of the Bureau of Labor Statistics) that could not be paid off by the brother. Such a large unpaid debt began threatening Russo's Seafood directly, so Charlie began working as a truck driver himself to pay down the debt before the bank began looking into the business's assets to cover the loss. The effort eventually paid off.

Charlie Jr., now head of Russo's Seafood, still wears his apron. He is in the shop at 6:00 a.m. every morning, save for one day that he takes for himself. You can still see him most days with his backward ball cap standing over the cutting table through the small window between the storefront that displays fresh whole mackerel, red snapper, whiting, flounder, grouper and others over ice. Other than a few select high-selling fish at standard cuts, which have been prepared prior to opening and wrapped for those in more of a hurry, Russo's customers select the fish and request specific size and cuts. The fish is then handed through the small window, and Charlie and his team quickly go to work scaling, cleaning and preparing the cut of fish to order. Charlie and his team are efficient and exacting if not surgical. They have near unmatched knife skills. Such are the skills of Charlie Russo that he is one of the very few fishmongers who has the closely held secret skill set to provide customers with boneless shad.

The American shad is one of the most underrated fish in Georgia. Shad is not just bait for big catfish anglers; it is part of the herring species and, as such, is very high in the all-important omega-3 fatty acids. So rich in omega-3 is shad that it may contain as much as twice the amount per weight as wild salmon. This Atlantic fish, which swims up Georgia rivers to spawn starting in January and through early spring (and up the rivers of more northern states as late as summer), happens to also be very low in toxins and mercury. And while this may not be a commonly known fact today, the founders of this country were well aware of the value of this delicious fish. Both George Washington and Thomas Jefferson were part of shad fisheries before and after the American Revolution.

Shad may have lost a lot of its popularity due to the number of small bones involved. Some chefs and cooks have tried to overcome this issue by soaking the fish in buttermilk in order to soften the bones. However, to avoid all of the difficulties with removing or softening those small bones, one need only go to Russo's Seafood and simply pick up some boneless shad. Regardless, with a season of only a few months, one has to wait until late winter/early spring for this treat.

Nostalgia washes over Charlie Russo when he recites stories of his grandfather taking a horse-drawn carriage down to the Ogeechee River for their preferred spot for shad. It doesn't take long, though, before nostalgia turns to frustration as Charlie recounts traveling to Atlanta to testify against the DNR's then new regulation efforts to control commercial shad and sturgeon fishing in the Savannah, Ogeechee and Altamaha Rivers, among others. Charlie sought to allow some more room in the regulation for the local commercial fishermen and fishmongers to provide locals who have lived on these fish for generations. The regulations passed despite Charlie's (and others') efforts to the contrary. One can nevertheless still get the regulated fish, but at higher costs and in much more limited quantities.

And while there have been other federal regulations that have also drastically changed where and how Charlie gets the fish to the store, it hasn't been all gloom and doom. Charlie Russo Jr. appears on all accounts to be a very happy man. He does what he loves and has loved since he was six years old. He does clarify, however, that he did not work with his father his entire career. After graduating from Savannah's Benedictine Military School, Charlie Jr. spent some time salmon fishing in Alaska. Thus, it seems when Charlie wasn't cleaning and carving fish, he was catching them.

He laughed when asked about the date he took over Russo's from his father. There appears to be no official date; his father simply did less and less as Charlie Jr. took on more and more. Charlie Jr. was running the shop for at least fifteen years before his father finally retired.

But from his first moments standing on a bucket to reach the cleaning table at the age of six until today, Charlie has noticed some changes in the market and the demands made on it. Transportation and shipping ability has, of course, greatly increased Russo's ability to provide guests with the freshest fish possible. It has also given Charlie the ability to provide guests with specific non-local and less popular fishes upon request. It's more than that, though. With Savannah's growing transplant population, Russo's has experienced an increase in demand for northern and international seafood— New England clams, Maine lobsters, octopus and Norwegian salmon, all of which the shop now carries fairly regularly.

Although the transplants to Savannah may seek out seafood from the North, native Savannahians are still enjoying the fare *de la mer*, the way they always have. Fried whiting, Sapelo Island clams, boneless shad, oyster roasts and wild Georgia shrimp in various forms are found throughout Savannah but not always in its restaurants.

Whiting, while mostly a seasonal fish, is still one of the most popular fishes in the shop, as it has been since 1946. Charlie explained that whiting is the preferred fish for fry shops throughout Savannah and particularly among Savannah's black communities. Whiting was once considered a secondary sell for shrimpers in the Savannah area—the fish often being caught in the shrimper's nets. This meant that the meaty and tender fish was often cheap and readily accessible. However, as federal regulations aimed at protecting sea turtles began being heavily enforced, shrimpers caught less and less whiting. This, in turn, led to changing the manner in which whiting was acquired, and Russo's Seafood was more than happy to find suppliers for the Savannah demand.

Russo's Seafood may provide oysters to its customers from Apalachicola, Florida, and elsewhere, but that is not to say that Charlie is against the local oysters. To the contrary, Charlie still enjoys Savannah's delicious, sweet oysters as much as the native Creek tribes of the area did nearly ten thousand years ago. The brackish waters of Savannah's snaking rivers and creeks are perfect for oysters. As the tide shifts from high to low, many of the oyster beds reveal themselves. The Mississippian cultures, as they migrated east toward the coast, found these oyster beds toward Tybee Island (approximately eighteen miles east of Savannah) to be of vital importance. These first peoples—including Yamacraw, Muscogee and Euchee Nations—consumed the seafood not only for its protein but for its salinity as well. Salt was of vital importance during the summer given the heat and humidity that would draw out much of these early inhabitants' sodium from their pores. Replenishing electrolytes and sodium became a key survival tool. The salt reeds in the marshes of Tybee Island were also used for this purpose. In fact, the word *tybee*, as in Tybee Island (also nicknamed Savannah Beach), is believed to be the Euchee word for salt. The Euchees also used the shells of the oysters to build mounds in large ring patterns—believed to be ceremonial in nature, although it is a topic of research and debate to this day. These shell rings have been discovered all over the Lowcountry, with one of the largest and widest researched areas being on Sapelo Island (about one hour south of Savannah), a mound standing approximately 20 feet tall and over 255 feet in diameter.

Charlie, and many Savannahians, have chosen to relish in these local oysters through oyster roasts. This method of cooking may have become popular in Savannah because the local oysters tend to be in heavy clusters, making separating these oysters into individuals difficult. The easiest way to consume the native variety of oysters, according to Charlie, is to "roast" or steam the oysters. He explained that oyster roasts used to require building a large fire over which a metal (often tin) table was built, and large burlap bags full of oysters were thrown thereon. Today, most oyster roasts involve steaming oysters in a large pot, although Charlie assures us that many old-timers still roast oysters in more traditional methods. Savannahians traditionally wait until the cooler months—primarily between November and January—to start roasting oysters, as this is thought to be prime oyster picking time when the waters aren't above the ninety-degree mark.

Outside of roasting one's own oysters, there are surprisingly few places for one to enjoy roasted oysters in Savannah today. On the other hand, a relatively new hot spot in downtown, Sorry Charlie's Oyster Bar, roasts oysters from up and down the East Coast in a wood-fired oven. Sorry Charlie's Oyster Bar is on the corner of Congress and Barnard Streets, on the east side of Ellis Square, where the old City Market used to be. The casual oyster restaurant's building is not only one of the oldest commercial buildings in Georgia, but it also happens to be the building where Charlie Russo's great-uncle, Frank C. Mathews, operated his seafood market until it finally dissolved in 1998.

Following the close of Frank C. Mathews' Seafood, a small sports bar named Sorry Charlie's sprang up in the early 2000s in Frank's old seafood market. The owners of that Sorry Charlie's kept Frank C. Mathews's neon fish sign hanging until it fell due to high winds in 2006. The sign was eventually repaired, but when the old and largely neglected building was condemned in 2007, the bar closed and the building lay vacant and literally crumbling (some of the brick façade smashed against the sidewalk in 2012, requiring scaffolding to be erected) for nearly seven years. Harley Krinski, owner of one of Savannah's more successful nightclubs, the Social Club, along with his partners, bravely took on the challenge of restoring the historic building. With no raw bar and very few restaurants serving actual roasted oysters in the area, Harley and his team saw the opportunity to restore a Savannah tradition. In 2014, Sorry Charlie's was reborn as an oyster bar. In homage to the original seafood market in the same spot, the neon logo hanging over Congress Street includes the refurbished fish logo of Frank C. Mathews' Seafood (and now an officially delineated historic sign), which has been hanging over the street since 1947.

With so many Savannahians having enjoyed their seafood from Charlie Russo and his family (A.C. Mathews, Louis C. Mathews and Frank C. Mathews included) for the past one hundred years or so—including great Savannah restaurants like Elizabeth on 37th—it's fairly safe to say that Savannah's seafood does run through Charlie Russo's veins. And with all of his elder relative's locations having closed, we are all so very lucky that Russo's Seafood is still there.

CRYSTAL BEER PARLOR AND CRAB STEW

There are few places left in the world that fight to stay the same way they were in 1933. This might be for good reason. Eighty-four years ago, the United States was reaching the nadir of the Great Depression, and the world was barreling toward another global war. This greatest of all wars, as we now know, would be held on such an unfathomable scale that all of the wars since couldn't tally up a combined casualty list equaling that of World War II. It is by many accounts and in many respects one of the worst periods in human history. There were, however, a few bright spots in this period, as the jovial man sitting across the rich red booth in the dark but lively restaurant on the corner of Jefferson and Jones Streets remarked. Count Basie, Louis Armstrong and Ella Fitzgerald were starting to reach mainstream radio audiences. Savannah's own Johnny Mercer was heading west to take Hollywood by storm. Men and women's fashion was at its zenith in the United States. And of course, America's thirteen-year alcoholic beverage drought had just ended. A native Savannahian and avid collector of old photographs of long-since-gone local restaurants and other such Savannah iconography, John Nichols tries to keep the celebratory spirit of the end of Prohibition alive in one of the Lowcountry's most celebrated restaurants, the Crystal Beer Parlor.

As is often the case with anything dating back more than eighty years, the Crystal Beer Parlor is dripping with legends and myths—perhaps more so in this Savannah institution. It is rumored that the Crystal Beer Parlor was one of the first restaurants in the entire United States that legally served alcohol to its patrons following the ratification of the Twenty-First Amendment. It is similarly rumored that the Crystal was once a speak-easy. John Nichols admitted, however, that he has found nothing in the random collection of ancient barware and antique menus to actually prove either claim. Nevertheless, there is plenty of circumstantial evidence to keep the rumors alive.

In the early 1930s, William "Blocko" Manning and his wife, Connie, bought the old Gerken Family Grocery Store building. Julius Weitz and his parents had run the small grocery store since the early 1900s while they lived in the apartment upstairs. Blocko and his wife took the opportunity to live in the upstairs apartment while turning the grocery store into a small restaurant known as the Crystal Parlor. Given Blocko's previous incarceration for bootlegging and reports of meetings with Al Capone himself, it didn't take long for the rumors to start circling about the true purpose of the Crystal Parlor. Rumors weren't forgotten or even dissipated following the end of the Prohibition, when overnight the Crystal Parlor was renamed Crystal Beer Parlor. To the contrary, most saw the instant availability of alcohol at the repeal of the Eighteenth Amendment as something other than coincidental. Reports insinuated that the booze was already on the premises on December 5, 1933, and that not only the police but also the customers were aware of Blocko's ongoing bootlegging and speak-easy.

With the lifting of alcoholic prohibition, the Crystal Beer Parlor seemed to flourish. The restaurant became a local go-to for quality, fairly priced burgers and well-prepared local fare. The Mannings handed the ownership to their son, Ermine Conrad "Snookie" Thomson, who eventually handed the ownership over to his son, Conrad Thomson, the last in the Manning family line to own the Crystal Beer Parlor. Conrad, in trying to expand the restaurant to a second location, ran up debt to the tune of more than $2.2 million. The debt eventually caught up with him, and he was forced to shut down the expansion restaurant in 1999, followed by the original in 2000. After bank auction, the Crystal Beer Parlor was resurrected for a period of time until it, too, became insolvent.

This is where John Nichols enters the picture in 2009. John, a longtime caterer with successful runs of small restaurants with his brother, was not

Early 1930s photo of Henry Gerken Family Groceries store and family, with bicycle, in front of the store. *Courtesy of John Nichols.*

The original owner of Crystal Beer Parlor, "Blocko" Manning, with his wife inside the bar. Circa 1933. *Courtesy of John Nichols.*

originally interested in the property. At the urging of his staff and locals alike, John took another look and saw the establishment for what it was: a Savannah standard. Upon taking the challenge to breathe new life into the Crystal, John—taking a cue from his famous uncle, Mayor John Rousakis (known for revitalization and renewal of downtown Savannah in the late 1970s and 1980s)—painstakingly refurbished and reclaimed the bar. This is when John noticed the trapdoors—two under the bar floor and one in what is known as the Monroe Room—that led only to dirt, further fueling speculation that Blocko Manning had, at the very least, stored booze at the restaurant during Prohibition.

Nichols, who started his culinary career serving at Savannah's oldest restaurant, the Pirates' House, would in 2009 become the most successful owner of Savannah's second-oldest restaurant. He knew the restaurant had a lot of history, but not all of it was good. He remembered that the Crystal Beer Parlor from the 1960s was a place where his father would jump out of the car to grab some burgers to go—it was not a place for families. It appears from some accounts that it was not a place for ladies, either. In fact, it was not until after World War II that the restaurant served its first woman, Cornelia McIntyre Hartridge, mother of Connie Hartridge, a Savannah socialite, designer and fourth-generation owner of the Battersby-Hartridge House on Charlton Street.

So, it was clear to John that success would mean making a few necessary changes while fighting hard to keep the essence of the original product. While energy was put forth to make the restaurant more family-friendly and inviting, meticulous effort was given to returning the décor and furnishings to an appropriately 1930s ambiance. Moreover, John hired back some key staff members to help with continuity of product. He even went so far as to honor two forty-plus-year veteran servers by naming two of the rooms in the restaurant after them. To this day, one can request a seat in the Monroe Room, named after Monroe Whitlock, or the Smitty Room, named for A.G. "Smitty" Smith.

Among the many incredible efforts in bringing back the true Crystal Beer Parlor, John wanted to re-create the timelessness of the original menu. He drew his inspiration from unsurfaced old menu boards he found deteriorating in the storage shed. He had those menus restored, and they now decorate the southernmost wall of the Smitty Room. In this effort to re-create an authentic menu (for which there were no written recipes), John and his staff tirelessly tinkered at one of the Crystal Beer Parlor's greatest treasures: crab stew. This was a particularly good crab stew, and getting it right was essential. Longtime Crystal Beer Parlor patrons seem to agree that John and his team have successfully accomplished bringing the crab stew back to its former glory.

Crab stew—or she-crab soup, if you'd prefer—is not just a staple of the Crystal Beer Parlor. It is the glorious premier dish of Savannah itself. It's Savannah's Philly cheesesteak, Savannah's po'boy. Better yet, it's

SHORT ORDERS

STEAK
LIVER & GIZZARD
LIVERS
FRIED CHICKEN
FRIED SHRIMP
SHRIMP SALAD
FRIED OYSTERS
HAM OMELETTE
COLD PLATE
HAM & EGGS
HAMBURGER STEAK
FRIED POTATOES
SLICED ONIONS
FRENCH FRIED ONIONS
LETTUCE & TOMATO SALAD
CRYSTAL SPECIAL STEAK
LIVER & GIZZARD COUNTRY
BARBECUE
FRIED CHICKEN COUNTRY
BOILED SHRIMP
SHRIMP OMELETTE
OYSTER STEW
CHEESE OMELETTE
CHICKEN SALAD
BACON & EGGS
CHILI
FRIED ONIONS
SLICED TOMATOES

Original short-order sign of Crystal Beer Parlor, restored by John Nichols at Crystal Beer Parlor, York Street, Savannah, Georgia. 2016. *Donald Card.*

Savannah's clam chowder. Indeed, the delicate yet hearty broth is so representative of Savannah and Lowcountry cuisine that it is hard to find any dinner establishment that does not make its own version of the dish. It is fairly surprising, however, that such a careful balancing of the quiet flavor of blue crab with the sweet touch of sherry and cream is not an easy dish to find elsewhere in the country. It's a signature dish of Savannah that necessitates its own trip for anyone living outside the Lowcountry.

And yet the origins of Savannah's most famous of dishes lie far from its snaking rivers and marshy swamps. It lies much farther north and much farther east. Think Scotland. Think northeast Scotland. Think the frigid shores of the North Sea. Earliest recipes of such a crab-based soup date back to the early 1700s and are attributed to Scottish settlers in the brand-new province of Georgia and the Carolinas.

Yes, you read that right. "She-crab soup" or "crab stew" is actually Scottish in origin. It turns out that the Scots were hugely important to Savannah from its earliest colonial moments to modern times. As noted earlier, in 1734 a few of Oglethorpe's trustees were able to secure the support of 177 Scottish Highlanders—most of whom hailed from Inverness-shire in the northeast of Scotland and were known for their militaristic fortitude—to be the first guardians of this new settlement. By all accounts, these Highlanders were instrumental in securing Savannah's safety and assisting in the British war with the Spanish occupying what is now Florida. Throughout the 1700s, waves of immigration brought hundreds more Scots to both Georgia and the Carolinas.

These Scots brought their traditions, culture and, of course, their culinary tendencies. Of their delicacies, the Scots introduced a dish called "partan-bree"—*partan* being the Gaelic term for crab and *bree* being the northeast Scottish dialect's pronunciation for "brew" and often used to refer to soup. Partan-bree is a traditional soup seen on the northeast coast of Scotland (from where Savannah's guardians were plucked), where the primary fishing communities are found. The earliest recipes describe a soup with heavy cream, rice and crabs. The rice in many of these recipes was used as a puree to thicken the soup into more of a bisque.

Partan-bree in Savannah became slightly different from the original recipe in that it did not contain rice. The change in the recipe was not one out of choice but likely necessity. Given the early age of the city and the failed experiment of the Trustees' Garden, rice was not as readily available or as cheap as it was in the Carolinas. It wouldn't be until the 1750s—some twenty years after the founding of the city—that the Salzburgers began producing rice in trade-worthy quantities. Therefore, rice was removed from the dish, and to this day, the soup is made with heavy cream and often thickened with flour rather than rice.

How partan-bree took on the name "she-crab soup," on the other hand, is a whole other story. In fact, it is several stories. More like legends and conjecture than anything definitive. If you are in Charleston, you may hear stories that start with President William Howard Taft's visit with Mayor R. Goodwyn Rhett in the early 1900s. Mayor Rhett is said to have asked his butler to "dress up" the pale crab soup that they usually served at banquets. The butler added the orange-hued crab eggs to give it color and add texture and a stronger flavor. In doing so, it is said that the butler used only the female crabs and the entirety of the female crabs (including her egg sac), which is why, according to some, the dish is called "she-crab" soup today.

However, in Savannah, female or "she-crabs" were hawked by vendors on the streets as late as the 1950s. Some accounts describe young women hiding bound she-crabs in headdresses. She-crabs, which were routinely returned to the water by fishermen upon returning with their catch so that they could lay eggs and maintain the sustainability of the crab, would often be quickly plucked by enterprising opportunists who would then sell them to whomever they could on the streets surrounding and throughout the City Market. It is argued that it would be in bad form to serve a female crab, so she-crabs would be shelled and served in soups, where the identity of their gender would be hidden.

The name carries on today, but you will not often see many soups with the crab roe or find many chefs who distinguish between using male or female crabs in the production of the soup. Most would have a hard time finding a

17Hundred90 Inn & Restaurant exterior sign and stairs. 2015. *Pablo & Brit Photography.*

distinction in flavor between a male or female crab, but the orange-red hue of a she-crab's eggs and egg sac is fairly distinctive way of determining if your soup is indeed a "she-crab" soup.

Many have also argued that the name she-crab soup is derived from the use of sherry as a way to sweeten the taste of the creamy, delicious, delicate and highly addictive soup, but there is little evidence to support this theory. Nevertheless, crab stew or she-crab soup is most often served either with sherry on the side, drizzled over the top or even cooked in the soup.

It is not just the Crystal Beer Parlor that is showcasing this dish, although it is likely the oldest Savannah recipe in any restaurant. Many restaurants throughout the city have either a she-crab soup or a crab stew on the menu. One such great example of this rich, filling soup is Miss Annette's Crab Stew at the hauntingly beautiful 17Hundred90 Inn & Restaurant on the corner of Lincoln and President Street.

And yet despite the Hostess City embracing the soup as one of its culinary signatures, most visitors to the area are unaware of its origins or whose recipe has been serving Savannahians the longest. With so much care put into making sure the Crystal Beer Parlor's crab stew is as authentic as the restaurant itself, guests can almost taste the effort. It has been not just the classic crab stew to which many restaurants in the area aspire. It is and has been the very flavor of Savannah since 1933.

BOAR'S HEAD GRILL & TAVERN'S SHRIMP AND GRITS

Somehow, the Boar's Head Grill & Tavern seems hidden on the busiest street in Savannah (River Street). Maybe that has something to do with it being upstairs from the bustling Savannah's Candy Kitchen. Or perhaps it's because the "Boar's Head" name leads some visitors to mistake the oldest restaurant on River Street for something connected with the New York–based deli meat company. Whether you spot it right away or whether it takes you some time to discover it, there is no doubt that you will find the restaurant to be special.

The heavy dark wood door opens to long wooden plank floors, charred brick and stone walls and windows that overlook the river and Hutchinson Island. It's quiet and almost minimalistic in décor. The thick walls keep Boar's Head Grill & Tavern cool and isolated from the sounds and excitement of River Street. With all of the souvenir shops, street vendors, bars, clubs and hotels up and down the neighborhood, the restaurant is like an elegant oasis.

From all accounts, it was more of an oasis for the first twenty-odd years of its existence. As mentioned previously, River Street wasn't always bustling with tourists. The riverfront was teeming with business from the early 1800s until 1919 with cotton activity. After the American Revolutionary War general (and "Savior of the South") Nathanael Greene died of heatstroke while tending to his Savannah cotton plantation awarded to him for his war efforts, Caty Greene (his wife) sought the help of a Massachusetts tutor by the name of Eli Whitney to assist her with educating her children. During his time at the Greenes' Mulberry Grove Plantation, Eli Whitney took it upon himself to analyze the extremely tedious and inefficient cotton processing at the farm. The separating of the cotton from the sticky seeds was done by hand and would take hours with multiple hands to make a bushel. In 1794, Eli filed his patent for the cotton gin, which was eventually validated in 1807. Almost instantly, the cotton industry blossomed, with production exponentially increasing; due to patent infringement (as a result of the rather early stage of patent enforcement in the United States) and an unpopular sales scheme, though, Eli Whitney did not benefit as much from the invention as he originally anticipated.

Contrary to Whitney's mediocre success from his invention, the cotton industry boomed in Savannah as a result of the gin. More cotton warehouses along Savannah's riverfront were built in the early 1800s, and by 1817, the need for cotton factors (similar to modern-day brokers) had grown. Savannah soon became the cotton hub of the South. The cotton factors built their offices atop the existing cotton warehouses and, by 1886, had built the Cotton Exchange to better factor and price the cotton. The industry continued to flourish for another thirty years or so following the construction of the Cotton Exchange until disaster struck. A cotton-plant eating pest known as the boll weevil decimated the cotton plantations in 1919, and a few years later, there was nothing left on Savannah's riverfront. The years leading up to and following the Great Depression meant that the warehouses and offices remained empty. Windows were boarded up. Businesses had long left. The tight, dark alleys and walkways under the Factors' Walk became hangouts for the homeless and those with dangerous intentions. It remained more or less in this state until Mayor Rousakis instituted his urban renewal projects in 1979.

As Brenda Anderson (co-owner of Smith Brothers Butcher Shop) put it, Savannah's River Street was just not a nice place to go. There was, as it turns out, one exception. In 1959, Boar's Head Grill & Tavern opened its doors on the corner of Lincoln Street ramp and River Street. It is important to note that the sign that hangs over River Street incorrectly dates the restaurant to 1964—a full five years after its inception. It is uncertain why the previous owners cut five years off the life of the restaurant, but the restaurant clearly dates back to before 1964. At the very least, we can prove that the restaurant existed in 1962, as it was a set location for *Cape Fear*, the film starring Robert Mitchum. Conspicuously, the eerie ambiance of Savannah's riverfront in those days played into the scene where Robert Mitchum's character lures a young woman from the bar.

Today, Chef Philip and Charlene Branan provide an exceptional dining experience that honors the history and heritage of the restaurant and the riverfront of Savannah. They have owned the restaurant for more than eighteen years now. Charlene was born and raised in Savannah, where her family has been in the restaurant business for two generations. Philip Branan had an apprenticeship with the famous Atlanta-based restaurant group Pano & Paul and went on to study at the Culinary Institute before becoming the head chef at the Ritz Carlton in Naples, Florida. Philip believed that he would never realize his full potential unless he was operating his own establishment, and so the couple returned to Savannah and began the hunt for a restaurant. Philip and Charlene, who have known each other since Charlene was fifteen years old, settled on purchasing the Boar's Head restaurant from the retiring owners and transforming the menu to the spectacular fare it offers today.

Food is at the center of the Branans' life. When he is not in the kitchen producing award-winning dishes, Chef Philip is tending to his bees or raising his own organic produce at his farm in nearby Statesboro (one hour west of downtown). Whenever possible, Chef Philip will provide seasonal produce to his restaurants, not because it is trendy to be a farm-to-table restaurant but because it genuinely makes his dishes better. The restaurant does not advertise as farm-to-table, and it doesn't market itself with dishes made from organic produce. The food should delight the palate first and foremost. Everything else is secondary.

Chef Philip's dishes have won awards and praises throughout the city. His chocolate bread pudding is considered the "best dessert in Savannah," and his bacon-wrapped barbecue shrimp, which actually features a peach-based barbecue, has also won much praise. And while Chef Philip's rendition of shrimp and grits haven't won any awards yet, it is this dish that first drew our attention to Boar's Head. It is a stunning dish. It is highly addictive. It deserves a clean palate and a healthy appetite.

Shrimp and grits is one of the more popular dishes in the South. Many restaurants prepare a version of the dish, and many southern households serve this meal on a somewhat regular basis. The dish is quite frankly simple; it really only requires two ingredients. The basic dish is seen in a very real way as a blank canvas on which to build a masterpiece. In fact, building one's own distinctive shrimp and grits dish has become a hot topic in the Savannah area, with many places—especially in the catering sector—offering build-your-own shrimp and grits bars. *Southern Living* magazine hosts Jekyll Island's (approximately two hours south of Savannah) annual Shrimp & Grits Festival. This festival, usually held in the second week in September at the height of the main shrimping season, highlights the Lowcountry's love affair with this dish, as well as its broad appeal far beyond the marshes.

With so many versions of the dish out there in restaurants and homes, it begs the question as to why one should get shrimp and grits at Boar's Head Grill. But the answer is actually quite simple. Boar's Head Grill's shrimp and grits is flat out delicious. It is carefully constructed with superior ingredients like wild Georgia shrimp, featuring a well-balanced flavor profile that does not overwhelm guests with spices that mask the sweet succulent shrimp and creamy grits. It also doesn't pretend to be a dish that it is not; it need not be more sophisticated than literally the two ingredients in its name. That being said, there are many great places in Savannah to get mouthwatering shrimp and grits, like Tondee's Tavern's white wine reduction with bacon shrimp and grits or Olde Pink House's shrimp on cheesy grit cakes. You should try the dish everywhere in the Lowcountry. And you should definitely order the dish at Boar's Head.

Many northern visitors are befuddled by grits, a dish not often seen in menus north of the Mason-Dixon line. Nevertheless, grits are among the first true American foods. They were introduced to early European explorers as something more along the lines of hominy—a kind of corn-based porridge, where the corn kernels were skinned but usually whole. It is said that Sir Walter Raleigh first "discovered" what we now consider grits while on a reconnaissance party on Roanoke Island in the Outer Banks of North Carolina—site of the Lost Colony. The dish was easy and filling, and with corn being easy to grow in the new colonies, hominy became a popular ration. Over time, the corn was ground coarsely, and European cooking techniques—principally the use of butter and cream or milk—changed whole-kernel hominy in the coarsely ground grits we know today.

Shrimp as a topping to grits is thought to relate directly to the fishermen and shrimpers of Georgia and South Carolina. There are some references to "shrimpers grits," which describe fishermen adding shrimp to their breakfast porridge, as there were few other available ingredients to add to a bowl of grits while out to sea. Regardless, as just about every protein has been added to grits at one point or another, it was only a matter of time before the Lowcountry latched on to this dish, one now served at any time of the day.

Georgians also like to point to their prized wild Georgia shrimp as the source of the popularity of the dish and argue that their neighbors to the west and north merely serve an imitation of the original. Shrimp in Georgia has always played a large part in the cuisine of the coast, and with wild Georgia shrimp considered some of the best, sweetest and most succulent shrimp in the world, one can forgive Georgians for a little braggadocio. So many of the world's shrimp are farmed, but wild Georgia shrimp are born out of the estuaries with water filtered by the marshes off the Atlantic coast and subject to the tides. This is why the superiority of the wild Georgia shrimp is often argued.

Its superiority aside, shrimp has always been an important part of Savannah's cuisine. With the failure of the communal gardening experiment, early settlers had to depend on what they could fish out of the waters to survive. Even when the plantation system began to take hold in Georgia, both the American Revolution and the Civil War saw the mouth of the Savannah River blockaded by enemy ships, preventing many of the foodstuffs from making their way to port. During these periods, Savannah's residents would once again depend on sustenance from the water for food, and with a long shrimping season (about March to the end of December), shrimp helped keep Savannahians fed.

Wild Georgia shrimp don't feed just Savannahians nowadays. The Georgia shrimping industry is part of the United States' seemingly insatiable appetite for shrimp. More than 650 million pounds of shrimp are harvested in the United States every year—far exceeding the demand in any other country, including much more populous and seafood-rich countries like China. This, as it turns out, still does not meet the demand for shrimp, requiring the United States to import another 250 million pounds from overseas (and mostly farm-raised). Although we have not been able to prove it, there is much evidence to suggest that the addictively rich shrimp and grits from Savannah's Boar's Head Grill is a major contributor to the American demand for shrimp.

Chapter 4

THE ART OF MAKING BREAD

Famed chef James Beard once remarked that "good bread is the most fundamentally satisfying of all foods; and good bread with fresh butter, the greatest of feasts." This wisdom, laid down in his book *Beard on Bread*, would have seemed like a tease to the residents of Savannah in the 1700s, as they struggled to make bread in the early days of the colony. Overcoming humidity, supply shortages and other difficulties were essential to Oglethorpe, who recognized that history has demonstrated that making and consuming bread has been one of the lynchpins for the development and sustainability of society. During the Middle Ages, there were only two commodities that were deemed essential to maintain civility: bread and beer. As a result, regulations were put in place to keep the peace. Governments of the Middle Ages instituted the "laws of bread assize." These laws governed everything from purity and grade of flour to the weight of baked loaves and even the price. Georgia founder James Oglethorpe and his trustees enacted their own bread assize laws while laying out their plan for the colony.

Oglethorpe not only adopted the medieval practice of regulating bread, but he also added in his own strict policies of oversight. Early Georgia bakers were required to be open for inspection by the justice of the peace at any time. This applied to the bakeries as well as the bakers' private homes. If there was ever a complaint of a baker not following the strict rules set forth in the law, justices of the peace could easily figure out which baker created the substandard loaf due to the bakers' identification mark that would have been required on every loaf sold.

These assize laws were meant to make sure that everyone was fed and had their proper share of life-sustaining bread. However, and rather unexpectedly, it was Oglethorpe's prohibition of slavery in Savannah that compounded the bread issues. One of the unintended consequences of Oglethorpe's slavery ban was a shortage of bricks and, thus, a shortage of ovens. Because brick-making was typically the job of slaves, and Savannah had banned slaves, the lack of bricks meant that having ovens in every home was nearly impossible. The solution to the brick problem was found in another medieval practice: communal ovens.

While a blessing to the everyday residents of early Savannah, the communal ovens just off Johnson Square were a bane to any professional baker trying to make a living in the new city. Early residents used the ovens to not only make their dinners but also bake their own homemade breads. The square even took on the nickname "Bakers Square" due to all the locals making their own breads and baked goods. With the growing availability of flour to the regular man and strict assize laws, early professional bakers found it hard to make ends meet, let alone make a profit.

There was even more to contend with than just societal woes for early Georgian bakers. The hot, humid summers caused doughy loaves to stick together (altering the precise measurements of the loaves) or cause the bread to spread, obscuring the bakers' mark. Regardless of the reason, if reported to or noticed by a justice of the peace, the offending baker would be subject to harsh fines, which included monetary punishment and confiscation of all baked goods.

Many of these issues were alleviated and the shackles holding down the common baker removed when the Trustees' Charter ended in 1752 and, with it, the assize laws. Ever since this marquee moment, Savannah and the Lowcountry have had a love affair with bread and the bakeries that prepare them. Today, locals and visitors alike can enjoy the multitude of great bakeries across the city—from the incredible pastries and fresh-made bread at Our Daily Bread on Wright Square to Goose Feathers on Ellis Square to Back in the Day Bakery down on Bull and Fortieth Street. As great as these bakeries are, only a few baked goods companies have survived the test of time so far.

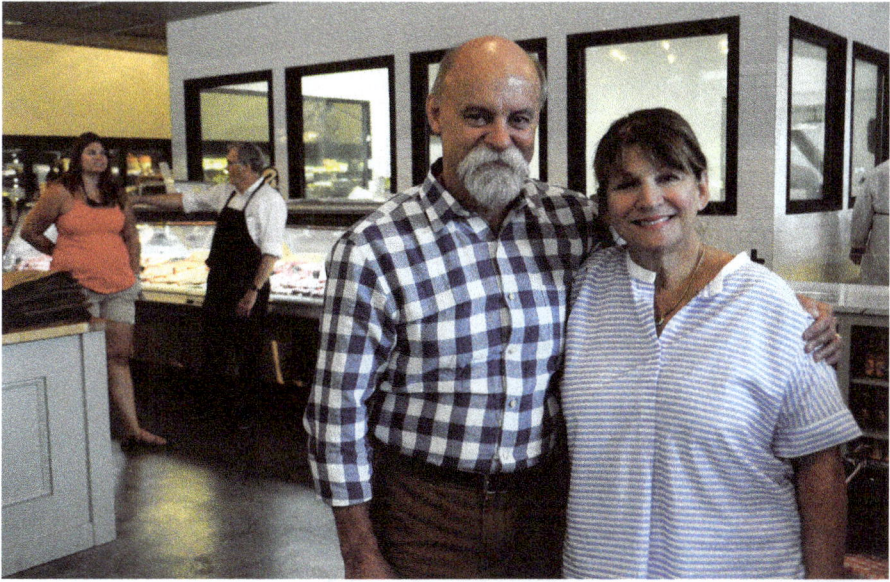

Above: Brenda and Robert Anderson, owners of Smith Brothers Butcher Shop in their Liberty Street, Savannah store. 2016. *Donald Card.*

Below: Boar's Head entrance and cobblestone ramp to River Street, with restaurant awning noting, "Est. 1959," while the wood-carved sign notes, "Est. 1964." River Street, Savannah, Georgia. 2016. *Donald Card.*

Left: Charlie Russo Jr. preparing salmon for a customer at Charlie J. Russo's Seafood, East Fortieth Street, Savannah, Georgia. 2016. *Donald Card.*

Below: Sapelo Island clams at Charlie J. Russo's Seafood. Savannah, Georgia. 2016. *Donald Card.*

Above: John Nichols, owner of Crystal Beer Parlor, York Street, Savannah, Georgia. 2016. *Donald Card.*

Below: Bowl of Georgia White Shrimp and Grits from Boar's Head Grill & Tavern, River Street, Savannah, Georgia. 2016. *Donald Card.*

Above: Gottlieb's chocolate chewies, a sort of brownie cookie. 2016. *Donald Card.*

Below: Ribs on smoker of Randy's BBQ shack on Liberty Street. 2016. *Donald Card.*

Collard greens, sweet potatoes, oxtail and corn bread from Sisters of the New South on Skidaway Road. 2016. *Donald Card.*

Teresa Weston, owner of Walls' BBQ, in her kitchen on York Lane. 2016. *Donald Card.*

Above: Looking west down York Lane toward Walls' BBQ. 2016. *Donald Card.*

Below: Beehives busily working on Canewater Farm, Carnigan, Georgia. 2016. *Donald Card.*

Above: Canewater Farm house seen through the pines, oaks and palm trees on the marshes of creeks leading out to the Altamaha River. 2016. *Donald Card.*

Below: A view of Cha Bella, a restaurant that focuses on local and organic ingredients, from East Broad Street. 2016. *Donald Card.*

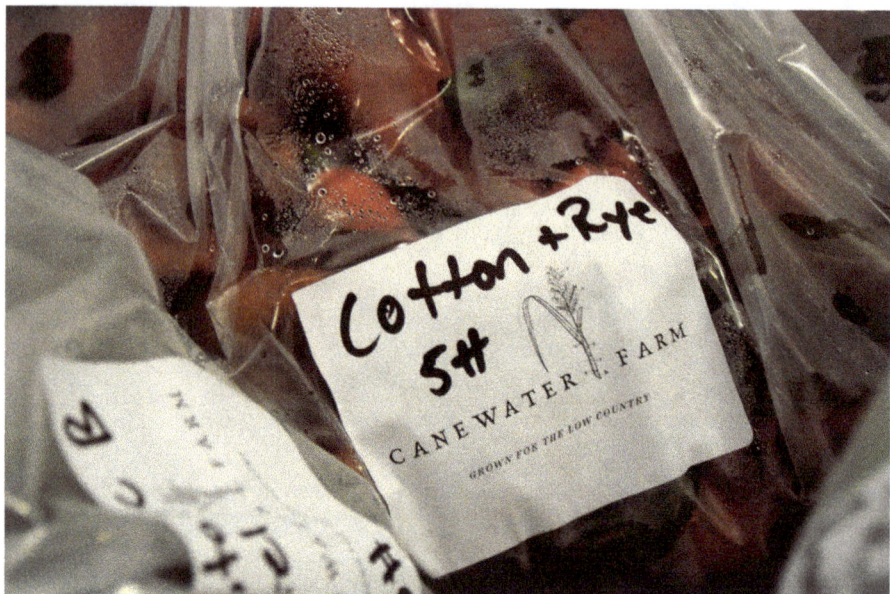

Above: Cotton & Rye's produce, ready to ship at Canewater Farm. 2016. *Donald Card.*

Left: Eggplant nearing its picking at Canewater Farm. 2016. *Donald Card.*

Above: Aged steaks and cuts of beef at Smith Brothers Butcher Shop. 2016. *Donald Card*.

Below: Sausage pies and other baked pastries in a display case at the British Pie Society. 2016. *Donald Card*.

Above: Farmer Rafe, his dog (Waylon) and his tractor. 2016. *Donald Card*.

Right: An assortment of sausage and pickled vegetables presented on a butchers block at Smith Brothers Butcher Shop. 2016. *Donald Card*.

Opposite, top: Walker Farms roasting onions and potatoes on display at Smith Brothers Butcher Shop. 2016. *Donald Card*.

Opposite, bottom: Refrigerated rows of fresh produce on the shelves at Smith Brothers Butcher Shop. 2016. *Donald Card*.

The bar and main seating area of the Crystal Beer Parlor. 2016. *Donald Card*.

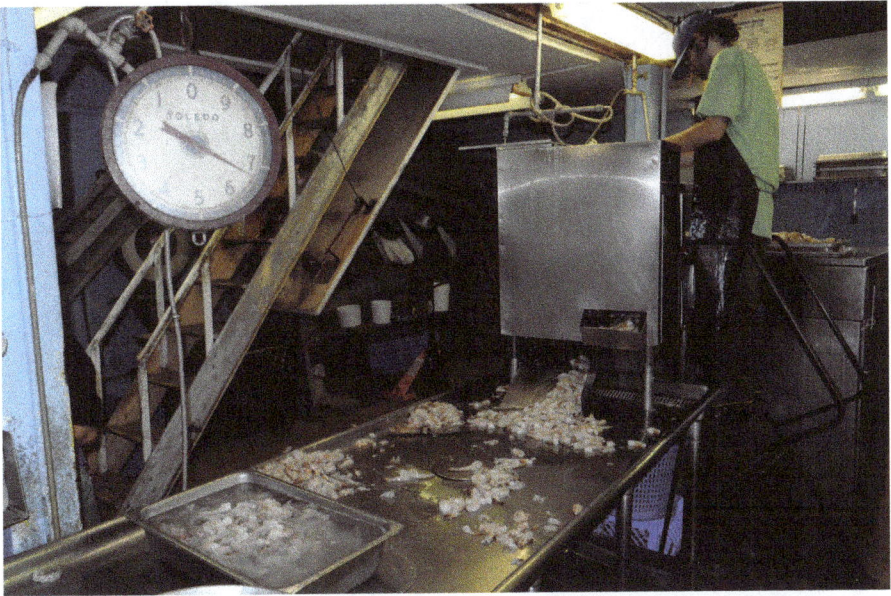

An employee at Russo's Seafood operating the shrimp peeler. 2016. *Donald Card.*

Line of hungry customers waiting outside Randy's BBQ shack. 2016. *Donald Card.*

Michael Lacy (owner/chef of Cha Bella) and Candice Carver (catering coordinator for Cha Bella). *Michael Lacy.*

Georgia White Shrimp Risotto at Cha Bella. 2016. *Michael Lacy.*

Right: Ted Dennard taking a rest between the beehives in the forest. *Savannah Bee Company*.

Below: Ted Dennard holding a hanging hive covered in bees. *Savannah Bee Company*.

Illuminated Byrd's cookie sign located at the Byrd's Famous Cookies museum. 2016. *Stuart Card*.

A hearty bowl of crab stew from Crystal Beer Parlor paired with corn bread and salad. *Jon Nichols*.

GOTTLIEB'S BAKERY

When Swiss medical student Johannes Hofer first coined the term *nostalgia* in 1688, he noted that the then-considered mental illness could be so debilitating that some suffering deeply had been known to die from the condition. Today, we no longer consider this longing for days gone by as a mental illness. Instead, we think of the sentimentality as a positive one. It's a way to give our past some perspective and our future some direction. This would appear to be the main emotion driving Michael and Laurence Gottlieb as they try to resurrect Gottlieb's Bakery. Their family's bakery was a cherished Savannah pastry shop that sold warm, toasty treats from 1844 to 1994.

The Gottlieb brothers grew up in the bakery that, at the time, sat on the corner of Bull and Broughton Streets. The boys were still in college studying culinary arts when their father, Isser Gottlieb, decided it was time to retire. The offer was made for the young men to take over the shop and continue on with the family legacy. After a lot of thought and soul-searching, both sons' desires to forge their own independent culinary identities led them away from the family business. In October 1994, much to dismay of the locals, the bakery closed it doors.

For more than twenty years, the lovers of Gottlieb's chocolate chewies and sweet rolls found no relief for their cravings. Then, after years establishing himself as a world-class fine dining chef, Michael Gottlieb ended his tenure with Omni Hotels and returned to his roots in the Savannah area. The opportunity arose to take over a small barbecue restaurant in Bloomingdale, Georgia (twenty minutes west of Savannah); Michael jumped at the chance to dress up southern barbecue. It also was the perfect opportunity to enlist his brother Laurence's help with doubling the kitchen space as a small bakery to bring back their namesake pastries.

The Gottlieb boys got right to work redoing the menu for Wood's Kitchen in order to wow its customers with locally sourced and creatively prepared casual dishes. At the same time, they started prepping the kitchen to double as a bakery in the wee hours before the restaurant opens. They began immediately cranking out delicious pastries and breads using the family's ancient recipes that won them the love of Savannah's locals in the first place. Places like Smith Brothers Butcher Shop in downtown Savannah wasted no time setting up a deal to sell Gottlieb's goods. Michael and Laurence hope that Savannahians and visitors alike will fall back in love with their delicious treats after finding them in these boutique food stores. They hope that as their popularity grows, the opportunity to once again have a Gottlieb's Bakery in downtown Savannah will be realized. Until then, these two passionate chefs are converting more space at Wood's Kitchen to amp up their wholesaling efforts. They are the fourth generation of Gottlieb boys to bake under their great-grandfather's brand.

It could be nostalgia for Gottlieb's that brought back the bakery's loyal customers after a more than twenty-year hiatus, but some credit must be given to the art of breadmaking that had been perfected in this family for more than one hundred years. Technique, skill and recipes handed down from generation to generation just makes Gottlieb's better. It all began with a young Russian Jewish boy, Isadore Gottlieb. Isadore traveled to the United States with his aunt and uncle in the early 1880s, escaping the clutches of pogroms, a series of persecutions and executions of Jews in Russia and eastern Europe during that time. In just three years' time, more than two hundred separate anti-Jewish riots and events occurred across what is now Ukraine and Poland after the assassination of Tsar Alexander II. The assassination was blamed by many on "the Jews." The first wave of these pogroms occurred between April and December 1881 and claimed the lives of forty Russian Jews, along with 225 reported rapes of Jewish women. The violence and animosity led to an exodus of Russian Jews from the 1880s until 1910.

Many of those who fled wound up in large cities with thriving Jewish communities like Chicago, New York and Boston. Although not as large, Savannah also opened its arms to the persecuted and poor Europeans. The cotton industry era was providing plenty of work and goodwill in Savannah at that time. In addition to the economic position Savannah provided, it also boasted its own Jewish community that dated back to 1733 and the first ships arriving in the new colony. In fact, the third-oldest congregation in the entire country, still with a temple on Gordon Street in the Historic District, is the congregation of Mickve Israel.

While many other immigrants found work in the bustling textile industry, Isadore Gottlieb chose a different path. At sixteen years old, this enterprising young man began baking traditional Jewish and Russian goods, which he peddled on the streets. Business was good, as fellow Jews and immigrants welcomed the deliciously familiar tastes of home. At the same time, lifelong Savannahians welcomed Isadore's skill and the flavors of international cuisine.

As Isadore's business grew, so did his family. He met and married fellow Russian immigrant Jennie and shortly thereafter began expanding his family. When it was all said and done, Mr. and Mrs. Gottlieb had six sons and two daughters. The young Isadore kept his family fed with his bakery operation, which was continuing to grow as quickly as his family. When the children were still young, Isadore would handle every aspect of his operation. His small bakery sat on the corner of Bryan and Montgomery Streets at that time. Here he handled everything from baking to bookkeeping and delivering the bread. In the early days, all deliveries were made on foot until the success of the business allowed Isadore to purchase a horse, Tom, and a trusty carriage. Tom was a superb worker: it is reported that when any of Isadore's young sons, who were not as familiar with the route as their father, went to make the daily deliveries, they could simply command, "Get up, Tom!" and the horse would would take them straight to the first stop. After each stop, they would repeat the command, and off the horse would go to the next stop. The children remarked that they knew when all of their deliveries were done for the day when horse returned to the bakery.

From the beginning, Gottlieb's was more than just a bakery. It was an institution, a pillar of the community. The bakery and Isadore provided Russian immigrants with their baked goods and the news at the same time, keeping the community informed. Many immigrants were unable to speak English let alone read it, so Isadore would translate the news into Russian for his customers during his deliveries.

Throughout the years, the bakery moved around from location to location as the descendants of Isadore continued the family tradition, occasionally adding to the family recipe book as they perfected the art of all things baked. Hank (one of Isadore's sons) became known for his fruit and oatmeal cookies. Others made cinnamon rolls and Washington pie, a sort of pudding made from bread, rolls, raisins, milk and eggs. When Isser shuttered the doors in 1994, chocolate chewies were the bakery's best seller. Many locals remember them and are welcoming them back as Gottlieb's more than one-hundred-year torch is slowly rekindling.

CLARY'S CAFÉ

It is fair to make the argument that Clary's Café is not a bakery, per se. Indeed, this most classic of all Savannah greasy spoon diners actually spent most of its existence as a drugstore and soda fountain—Clary's

Drugstore, as it was known then. Moreover, it is easy to enjoy a fantastic Hoppel Poppel breakfast (scrambled eggs, potato and salami) without ever noticing the homemade pies. Nevertheless, since the 1970s, it is likely that Savannahians and visitors alike have had more biscuits and homemade pie from Clary's than anywhere else in the city. With so many seasonal pie recipes and a fairly famous bread pudding, Clary's Café certainly earns a spot as one of the best places in the city to explore Savannah's baking prowess.

By the mid-1930s, when Luther Clary opened his second drugstore location on Abercorn and Jones Streets (the current location of the café), changes came quickly for the drugstore. Unfortunately, Luther passed away rather unexpectedly shortly after opening the Abercorn location, leaving his devastated wife, Clara, and daughter, Betsye, to manage the stores. Shortly thereafter, the original Clary's Drugstore on Perry and Bull Streets was closed, and the Abercorn location began selling more and more sandwiches and became known more for the soda fountain aspect than for the drugstore aspect. Although still referred to as Clary's Drugstore, by the time Clara sold the soda fountain in the 1970s, it was primarily a breakfast and lunch counter.

Clary's remained mostly a locals' counter until the mid-1990s. The diner, after all, is nestled in a residential part of the city, on the corner of the picturesque Jones Street and just a few blocks from Forsyth Park's surrounding the Victorian District. It was the release of the John Berendt bestseller *Midnight in the Garden of Good and Evil*, detailing several encounters with colorful locals, that helped propel the legend of Clary's even further. The success of the book and movie drove more and more visitors through the diner's doors every year. In fact, while the 1994 book refers to Clary's as a drugstore—there are even references to the eccentric inventor Luther Drigger ordering Bayer aspirin with his eggs and bacon—the term *café* became a more apt descriptor for the store given its new flurry of visitors. It stuck. Very little in Clary's today resembles a drugstore, but the soda fountain is a favorite relic for locals and visitors alike. Another longtime staple of Clary's has been the pie case, displaying the day's freshly made pies and famous giant éclairs. For this reason, while it has received a lot of attention for Drigger's antics in John Berendt's book, as well as for its breakfast and lunch plates and pies, Clary's has quietly been Savannah's sweet treat spot for decades.

BYRD'S FAMOUS COOKIES

The year 1924 was an extremely important and productive one in the United States. J. Edgar Hoover became the head of the Bureau of Investigation (and would later transform that agency into the Federal Bureau of Investigation). Edwin Hubble discovered that the Andromeda nebula is actually a galaxy, the first visual proof of galaxies outside the Milky Way. IBM was founded. New York held its very first Macy's Thanksgiving Day Parade. And Ben T. Byrd Sr. packed up his Model T Ford with wooden crates and delivered his first batches of cookies to the old City Market in Savannah.

Perhaps not all of these events are as important as others in the pre–Great Depression era. Then again, each initiated a tradition that is still acknowledged some ninety-three years later. Hoover is practically synonymous with the FBI, as is Hubble with astronomy and space exploration. IBM and Macy's Thanksgiving Day Parade are two of the most easily recognizable brands and products in the United States today. And Byrd's Famous Cookies are not just synonymous with Savannah but

Original factory of Byrd's Famous Cookies, located on Norwood Avenue. Circa 1956. *Byrd's Famous Cookies.*

BT "Cookie" Byrd at the counter of the Cookie Shanty. Circa 1981. *Byrd's Famous Cookies.*

also delectable cookies that can now be enjoyed in the Delta Sky Club, at Universal Studios or at Neiman Marcus department stores.

Ben T. Byrd set his bakery apart with the passion and consistent perfection that he put into his baking. His small bakery was successful from the beginning, delivering to the local markets every day in his Model T Ford. It wouldn't be until his son, BT "Cookie" Byrd, was brought on board that the company really took off. It was "Cookie" Byrd's idea to pack the cookies into tins—in order to make them more transportable—that put the company on the map. Sticking with the theme of being transportable, their cookies would be made as bite-size treats, which was also well received by the cookie consuming public. Byrd's version of the Benne Wafer also played a role in the success of the company, as people fell in love with this unique southern cookie.

A Benne Wafer is small cookie made from sesame seeds. In fact, the word *benne* is the Bantu (an East African language) word for sesame. Like many other things, the sesame seed made its way over from East Africa being

Ben "Pop" Byrd Sr. (*left*), an unknown salesman (*middle*) and BT "Cookie" Byrd Jr. (*right*) checking out new equipment. Circa 1956. *Byrd's Famous Cookies.*

A storefront venture for Byrd's cookies, the Cookie Shanty. Circa 1981. *Byrd's Famous Cookies.*

carried by African slaves. The seed was planted extensively throughout the South. The seed has a nutty, sweet aroma with a buttery taste. When toasted, these qualities are intensified, giving it a flavor almost of almond or peanut butter. It is rich in calcium and vitamins B and E. The seed is also high in protein and contains no cholesterol. Versions of this have been around in the South for a long time, but Byrd's is something special and has the sales to prove it.

Cookie's daughter, Kay, was next to lead a new generation of Byrd's cookie makers. Along with her husband, Benny, the company grew enormously. They added popular new cookies like Key Lime Cooler, which was the first cookie to win "Dessert of the Year" at the NASFT Fancy Food Show. This sweet, sour and crunchy cookie has gone on to become Byrd's top seller.

After more than ninety years, Byrd's is still family owned and operated. Stephanie Lindley, the daughter of Benny and Kay, now sits at the helm. Stephanie has continued to help Byrd's grow into a national treasure with its roots, kitchens and headquarters in Savannah. To celebrate this baking company's local heritage, Stephanie opened up a retail shop inside the City Market, where locals and visitors can pick up these treasures by the bag, tin or mouthful.

With such a rich, long-standing baking history, locals and visitors have come to expect incredible baked goods in Savannah. Savannah's baking tradition is in great hands, as a new crop of passionate Savannah bakers—like Dee Gibson of Mabel's Cupcakes and her partner, Josh Holland, at Our Daily Bread, as well as the duo Cheryl and Griffith Day (James Beard nominees for Outstanding Baking) of Back in the Day Bakery—add their sweet signatures to the city's baking legacy.

Chapter 5

BARBECUE AND THE SOUL OF FOOD

Statistically speaking, Savannah is a black city. According to the last U.S. Census (2010), approximately 57 percent of the Savannah population considers themselves Non-Hispanic Black or African American. For comparison, the same U.S. Census calculates that only 12.2 percent of the nationwide population identifies as Non-Hispanic Black. This gives Savannah the honor of having the tenth-highest black or African American population by percentage in the entire United States—only 0.7 percent behind Montgomery, Alabama.

Knowing this information, a culinary tourist might expect to find a higher percentage of black-owned restaurants and specialty food shops here than in other cities in the United States, yet this does not appear to be the case. Many possibilities for this imbalance in representation in the restaurant industry exist, but whatever the reasons, it is most stark in Savannah's Historic District, the city's main tourist hub. Only a handful of black-owned restaurants can be found, and even then those restaurants can be difficult to physically find, like Walls' BBQ, located in an alleyway with no hanging or lit signage. Nevertheless, the impact of the cooking styles, flavors and techniques from the Gullah and Geechee people, as well as other descendants of slaves in Savannah, can be seen everywhere in the city and is an extremely important ingredient in the culinary makeup of Savannah.

"Yamacraw Market." Fahn Street, Savannah, Chatham County, Georgia. Circa 1939.
Frances Benjamin Johnston.

WALLS' BBQ

A young black girl and her mother entered the Kress Department Store on Broughton Street to enjoy a light meal at the store's lunch counter for the first time. The young girl, perhaps the age of five at the time, was curious about all of the white faces in the store. Despite having lived in Savannah her entire childhood, the young Teresa Weston had limited interaction with the white people who shared her city prior to that day in 1962. She does not recall any animosity or bitterness from anybody, only mild curiosity.

Teresa was too young to understand what had come before her but just old enough to realize that things were now different as her mother, Margaret Weston, ushered her westward beyond Habersham Street—the de facto dividing line separating white Savannah from black Savannah. The lines were so distinctive and well observed at the time that Miss Teresa doesn't remember that awful period of our history as being all that bad. She lived in a "black neighborhood" on East York Street just off Greene Square. Her church was the only black Catholic congregation in the city. She attended school at St. Benedict the Moor Catholic Church, which was private but nonetheless a "black school." For most of her childhood—even for several years following the end of legalized segregation—young Teresa's interactions with white people were primarily limited to the nuns who taught at her school. Other than a memory of asking her mother why a young white girl came out of one door at the doctor's office and why she and her mother had to go in a different door, Teresa does not have many memories of legally segregated Savannah.

While Teresa's memories of Savannah during this period may seem somewhat benign and perhaps unusual, another well-known figure seems to share a similar experience of what it was like during and right after segregation in Savannah. Supreme Court justice Clarence Thomas was born in Pin

A "colored only" section of the train station during segregation. *Courtesy of John Nichols.*

Point, Georgia, and moved to Savannah at age seven, shortly after his single mother's home burned to the ground. He and his brother moved into their maternal grandparents' Savannah home. The Thomas brothers attended Catholic school for a period before transferring and ultimately graduating high school from St. John Vianney Minor Seminary on the Isle of Hope (a few miles southeast of downtown Savannah). The Supreme Court justice once remarked during a speech at Palm Beach Atlantic University, "To my knowledge, I was the first black kid in Savannah, Georgia, to go to a white school. Rarely did the issue of race come up."

Teresa Weston and Clarence Thomas's segregation experiences in Savannah may not have been the norm, as evidence is clear that African American struggles occurred both before and after segregation. After segregation ended, things didn't necessarily get better right away for the black community. Unemployment among African Americans was very high, and downtown black-owned businesses shut down left and right as a result of government repurchasing of properties and revitalization projects that effectively forced tenants to move to non-downtown communities. Walls' BBQ was one of the only black owned and operated businesses that managed to survive this period, although most guests probably don't realize just how close this very special restaurant came to never existing at all. Walls' BBQ could easily have been Walls' Beauty Salon instead.

It all started when Teresa's enterprising grandfather Richard Walls ventured from his family's farm, Shad's Plantation, in Bellinger Hill, South Carolina (about fifteen minutes north of Savannah), in the 1950s looking for ways to supplement the farm income. He came across the property on York Street one house down from the corner of Houstoun Street and the shady Greene Square (named for the famed American Revolutionary War hero Nathanael Greene). Having never had any experience with renting, Mr. Walls chose to purchase the property instead of renting it like the vast majority of his neighbors did with their respective homes in the 1950s.

With a base of operations for a number of small enterprises now in Savannah, Mr. Walls built himself a woodshed in the back of the house abutting the alleyway (or what Savannahians call a "lane"). Once the shed was built, Mr. Walls began cutting and hauling wood from his family's farm and storing it in his shed in Savannah, where he would sell to the neighborhood along with some of the produce grown from his farm. Portions of the family farm began to be parceled off and sold in order to have ends meet. Eventually, Mr. Walls got to a point where he began to rethink his Savannah property.

So, one day in 1963, Mr. Walls sat Teresa's mother and grandmother down to discuss the financial situation of the family and the future of the property. His solution was a simple one: the woodshed would be transformed into another, more profitable, business. As this would be a family enterprise, he asked the Walls ladies whether they would like to own, develop and run a beauty salon or a barbecue restaurant. Given the South Carolinians' familiarity with slow-cooking pork and beef over wood-fired stoves on the family farm, there was really no other choice in terms of types of restaurants.

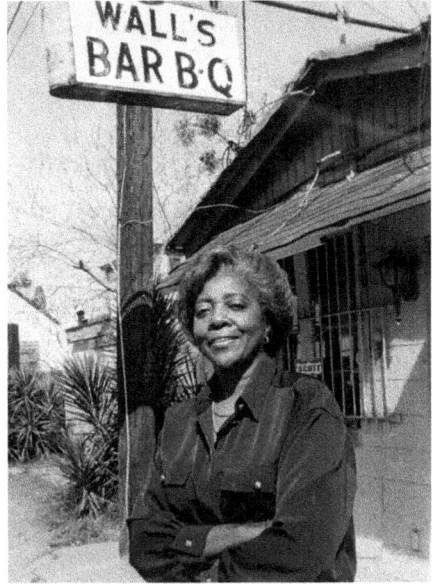

Margaret Weston (current owner Teresa Weston's mother) in front of the then hanging sign of Walls' Bar B-Q on York Lane, Savannah. The sign came down in a storm, and new city ordinances at the time prohibited its replacement. Circa 1996. *Walls' BBQ.*

It's a relief for all of us that the choice was barbecue, but more so for Teresa, who is just as excited today to carry on the family business as she was in the 1960s. Teresa is sure that it wasn't as close as a call for her mother and grandmother as it may appear. Margaret and her mother, Janie Walls, loved barbecue and cooking as much as her grandfather, and it turns out that there were few places in Savannah to get barbecue in those days. It just made more sense than a beauty salon.

There is a reason barbecuing speaks to most of us on a primeval level. The smell of meat sizzling over open flames is such an essential part of our species' survival that we are almost genetically structured at this point to crave barbecue. In fact, when the first Spanish explorers brought the concept from the aboriginal people of the Caribbean and what is now southern Florida back to continental Europe, *barbacoa*, the Spaniards' phonetic spelling of the native word, became an instant sensation both in Europe and in the new Spanish outposts throughout the New World. Linguists had deciphered the aboriginal language of the islands and what is now southern Florida, translating the term *barbacoa* to mean "sacred fire pit." With total U.S. sales of outdoor grills at more than $1.4 billion in 2016, along with tailgating events at an all-time high and nearly every weekend warrior firing up some charcoals or natural gas, it's fairly evident that the term hasn't lost any of its meaning over the centuries.

Since the 1700s, barbecuing has been very popular across southern states. There are several reasons for this, not the least of which was the availability of pigs. From Florida to North Carolina, where wild pigs and pig farming were most abundant, slow-cooking pork product over an open flame was ever-present. In modern times, regions across the South have been known for specific styles of barbecuing.

The coastal and Midland barbecuing styles of South Carolina most influenced Mr. Walls, given his upbringing. The upper South Carolina coastal barbecue, from the area also known as the "Pee Dee" region, is famous for its peppery vinegar sauce, which is used for whole hog roasting. The Midlands region of South Carolina is known for its "Carolina Gold" sauce—a mustard/vinegar sauce. Ms. Teresa's secret sauce, the recipe passed down from her South Carolinian grandfather and grandmother, seems to be a bit of both of these. Although she keeps the secret to the sauce, learned palates can detect traces of mustard and vinegar, as well as bit of sweet and pepper. Whatever it is, the sauce is highly addictive, and there is only one place in the world one can get it: a small shop down a dusty alleyway on the east side of Savannah.

And so in 1963, Miss Teresa's mother and grandmother began cooking family-favorite recipes for the neighborhood soon after the decision was made in favor of barbecue over beauty salon. The original restaurant offered no menus. Nevertheless, the neighborhood residents began to flock for their choice of ribs, crabs, fried chicken and French fries. The young Miss Teresa, only about six years old when the restaurant opened, helped in any way she could, but she wouldn't start really cooking for another five years. Teresa recalled the moment she first starting cooking earnestly with immense clarity and joy. Fed up with having to ask someone to make her favorite childhood dish—her grandmother's sweet potato pie—she decided to ask her grandmother to teach her how to make it so that she could have it whenever she wanted. Smiling, Miss Teresa noted that she hasn't changed the way she prepares this dish in nearly fifty years.

Teresa soon thereafter began mastering all of her grandmother and mother's recipes, with their help. Every attempt involved the taste buds and mentorship of her family—particularly that of her grandmother and a cousin who worked as a chef at the old DeSoto Hotel on Liberty Street. It was then that Teresa found her talent for dishes such as collards and other slow-cooked, stewed vegetables. She learned to set them, trust the recipes and leave them alone, sometimes for hours. Such patience and attention to detail made Teresa an integral part of Walls' BBQ kitchen team throughout her high school career. Her teenage years were spent in a rigid, self-induced schedule of attending school, working in the restaurant kitchen and studying.

By the time Teresa left to study at Howard University in 1974, the then eleven-year-old neighborhood restaurant was continuing to thrive. Although Teresa worried about how the restaurant would run without her, her parents supported her difficult decision to move to Washington, D.C., for her education. Teresa studied hard, but as she neared the end of her college career, she began to question her desire to spend the rest of her life working in the field of chemical engineering. In 1979, Teresa received word of her grandfather's death. Although she was just three credit hours shy of her degree, she knew where she needed to be. She would return to Savannah to be with her family.

Upon her return, Teresa recognized that her mother and grandmother required her help with the business. It was during this period, 1979–80, that Teresa started putting her stamp on the restaurant with the introduction of her family's version of popular dishes among black households in the area—like her grandmother's sweet potato pie, black-eyed peas and collard greens—as well as opening for lunch. The restaurant's clientele at this time was still mostly the black families from the Old Fort neighborhood and from east of Habersham Street, with the additional increase in occasional white guests stumbling a few blocks west from the then Fetchers Bar, which had popped up in 1979. Regardless of their background, all of the patrons learned of Walls' BBQ by word of mouth.

As things settled for her family, Teresa knew that she needed to complete her degree regardless of her intentions to practice in the field thereafter. She was wholly unaware that a movement had already begun in Savannah as she left for Howard University that would change the demographic makeup of the Old Fort neighborhood forever. By the time Teresa returned to Savannah with her degree in 1982, most of the black families who had rented their apartments and houses had moved. In their places were white investors who had taken the opportunities provided by the urban renewal projects put into effect by Mayor John Rousakis. Reportedly, some of these investors were able to buy properties in the neighborhood for as little as one dollar so long as they committed to so many thousands of dollars in renovations to the buildings. The transition in the neighborhood in such a short period was rather shocking to Teresa. Had it not been for Richard Walls's insistence on buying rather than renting the property where the restaurant sits, Teresa is convinced that Walls' BBQ would not have survived the neighborhood transition.

Despite the change in the neighborhood, Walls' BBQ continued to thrive. Longtime regulars took city buses from west Martin Luther King Jr. Boulevard and east of East Broad Street—essentially the entirety of Savannah's Historic District. The new locals immediately took a liking to the restaurant, and it continued on as it had always done, serving impeccably made home-style dishes for its patrons at reasonable prices.

Teresa split her time during this period between working in the restaurant alongside her mother and her other longtime passion, education, albeit this time as a teacher. As her mother required more and more assistance running the restaurant in the late 1990s, Teresa reluctantly retired from full-time teaching. She did, however, still do substitute teaching for the next twenty years or so and, in fact, still tutors today. Guests often remark on the small bookshelf full of calculus and geometry books, not realizing Miss Teresa's other passion is still being practiced.

Today, on a windless, relatively cool day in Savannah, you can smell the smoky sizzle of Miss Teresa's ribs for at least five blocks. It is hypnotic. Something primordial awakes in the soul as you get closer. If you know the location and which gravel dusted alleyway to wander down, the prize comes at the small building with a plastic corrugated awning and squeaky patio door. Find yourself a booth and peruse the menu. It is a familiar menu, but it is still very special.

The fact that this place is still around more than fifty-three years after it first opened is a huge testament to Teresa's cooking skills. Yes, Teresa Weston is the constant in the quiet east side neighborhood, once known as the Old Fort neighborhood, and this fact alone makes this place special. It is also true that Teresa has been the the smiling and welcoming spirit of Walls' BBQ for most of those fifty years—this fact also makes this place special in and of itself. One could make the argument that eating in a place that is an adventure to even find raises the experience, just as one could also argue that being served by the chef and owner heightens the enjoyment. All of these things are true, yet the bottom line in any restaurant is always the food. If the food doesn't cut it, the restaurant won't either. This is especially true when the restaurant doesn't market or advertise. Its success is purely based on great food and the power of word of mouth.

Teresa Weston tending to her pot in her Wall's BBQ kitchen. 2016. *Donald Card.*

Teresa is uncomfortable with the praise. She feels unworthy of it. She points to having only ever cooked in this one kitchen. She has no experience outside this place. She has no culinary training other than what her mother and grandmother bestowed. She even jokes that she graduated from the "KISS Academy of Cooking" (Keep it Simple, Stupid). As if to demonstrate this point, Teresa pointed to a large pot on her stove and remarked that she doesn't fuss over her food—the carefully selected ingredients, seasons and spices are added per recipe or memory, and then the food is left to just cook slowly. Perhaps unknowingly or perhaps just subconsciously, Teresa has just described, in part, the traditional cooking methods and techniques of the Gullah, Geechee and other local descendants of slaves—peoples who were forced to prepare their foods under low heat in the morning before setting out to work in the cotton fields and other such plantations of South Carolina and Georgia. This is a cooking method that is likely to lead to tender, well-blended dishes.

Specifically, Ms. Teresa's chopped pork is startlingly tender and moist. There is clearly some slow oven-cooking going on beyond anything done on her grill racks. Too often in smoke-blanketed barbecue joints throughout the South, chopped (or pulled) pork can be dry and tough. Not at Walls'. The pork spends time slow roasting in the oven so that some of the fat can keep the meat from drying up and the enzymes can be given the time to fully tenderize. It is plainly outstanding. This is nothing to say for smoky, delectable goodness of Walls' ribs or Teresa's favorite, sweet potato pie, or any number of incredible traditional dishes.

The food here is good because the dishes are timeless. It is all meticulously prepared by a traditionalist. There are no shortcuts taken. The food has been received as exceptional regardless of race or color or class, regardless of any culinary fad at whatever time over the past fifty years. The restaurant is one of only a handful of restaurants, in likely the entire world, that has survived for more than fifty years without changing ownership, without changing chefs and without marketing. And so perhaps the secret to all of Walls' BBQ recipes has been uncovered: a healthy pour of patience, a dash of trust in the recipe and three cups of experience, mixed in a small wood shed while gently folding in tradition.

THE INFLUENCE OF THE GULLAH AND GEECHEE

The origins of soul food and southern cooking in general can find their roots, like most distinguishable cuisines, in the people who worked the land and reaped its bounty. As the British debtors squandered their given plots of lands, failing in most cases to sustain themselves on the poor soil and brutally hot and buggy weather conditions in the summer months, demands for the repeal of the antislavery laws first established in the colony of Georgia started to grow. Those demands would be officially met on January 1, 1751.

It was argued that West Africa, from present-day Senegal down to Sierra Leone and into Liberia (known as the Windward Coast), would be the best place to find slaves most able to cope with hot summers and the conditions it breeds. Not only did the early plantation owners and slave traders feel that West Africans were physically suited for the position, but they also recognized the fact that there was a huge boom in rice, indigo and cotton just to the north in the Carolinas—these commodities are all indigenous to the Windward Coast. The slavers would drag not only the bodies of these enslaved Africans over to the Americas but also their ancestral knowledge of growing and cultivating highly valued crops.

Rice fields began to sprout up all along the Georgia and South Carolina coasts on the islands that dot its shoreline. The conditions were perfect for growing rice but not necessarily living, especially for the European landowners who were not as familiar with the heat and, moreover, the mosquitoes, sand fleas and other critters that enjoy a good nibble in the summer months. Malaria and yellow fever became endemic in the area, with the diseases being transported by the slaves from Africa. Having lived in a subtropical environment, West Africans had developed some immunity to these diseases. Europeans did not have this same resistance, and cemeteries started to fill with victims.

Fear of death from a mosquito-carried disease gave the slaves of the islands a little more autonomy than the slaves on other plantations. Most European landowners would leave the slaves in the hands of African "rice-divers," or overseers, on the islands, while they retreated inland, where some refuge could be taken from the elements. The lack of outside influence allowed these communities to retain much of their cultural identity.

During the Civil War, fear once again aided the slaves of the islands. This time, it was the fear of the U.S. Navy that led southern plantation owners to flee, abandoning their plots of land and the men, women and children who worked their fields. In 1861, Union forces arrived on the

"Going to market—a scene near Savannah, Georgia." Circa 1875. *E.A. Abbey.*

Sea Islands to find a people made virtually free already. It would be here, before the end of the war, where the first slaves in the South would be officially freed. Many chose to take up arms to fight alongside the North, while others stayed to form the first school for freed slaves on St. Helena Island.

These proud people are referred to as either Gullah or Geechee. While the name Gullah was given to these communities that lived on the islands off the Carolina coast, Geechee was given to the communities off the Georgia/Florida coast. Their cultures and language are separated and distinguished mainly by a small sliver of water. Gullah is often used as a blanket term for both cultures.

Many Gullah communities still populate the Lowcountry, but their people are now found nationwide, with communities building their own Gullah churches. Many of the freed blacks who once were forced into their labors refused to go back to work in the disease-ridden rice fields, so they picked up and moved elsewhere in search of a better life. Others moved away during a rash of hurricanes in the 1890s that destroyed homes and the crops that would support them. More recently, increased property value has led some to trade in their ancestral plots for profit.

Groups like the Penn Center, which is run out of that very same building that housed the first school for freed blacks, are actively preserving the heritage that laid the foundation of the South. With their help, the U.S. Congress passed the "Gullah/Geechee Cultural Heritage Corridor Act" in 2006. This provided $10 million over ten years to research, preserve and interpret historic Gullah sites.

One thing that preserved itself without the need of government intervention was the culinary dishes of the Gullah that worked their way into popular culture one taste bud at a time. If it has rice and some form of stewed vegetable, chances are it traces its roots to the Gullah. Gumbo, while most often associated with Louisiana, can most certainly trace its roots to the Gullah. The word *gumbo* itself means okra in the Umobundu language of East Africa. Anyone coming from Africa at that time most likely would have done so against their will through the southern ports of South Carolina and Georgia, right in the middle of Gullah country.

Anyone who has traveled to Savannah will have heard of Savannah red rice (just red rice to locals). This is arguably the most well known of all Gullah dishes. It is a prime example of how the original West Africans took what they knew and incorporated what grew around them in order to sustain themselves. Red rice is simply white rice cooked with crushed tomatoes instead of water, then celery, bell pepper and onion are added for seasoning; if you're lucky, some bacon or smoked sausage will set it all off. While original dishes would most likely not have contained much meat due to the situation in which the West Africans found themselves, the rest of the ingredients would have been grown in the communal gardens that the slaves would tend for their own sustenance. In doing so, they proved that a community gardening system could work in the sandy soils of coastal Georgia given the right knowledge and a skilled hand.

The contribution of the Gullah to Savannah's (and moreover the entire South's) culinary identity is undeniable. Perhaps the time-honored flavors of Gullah cooking are a testament to the resilience of the people who first stewed up these dishes. The ability to hold on to their roots after being dragged from their homelands to work the fields in hot and humid marshlands, separated by an ocean from all that they knew, is remarkable. It should be no surprise that a culture that built the foundations of our country is also responsible for the foundation of southern cuisine. Today, some of those traditions are proudly being carried forward in Savannah in incredible restaurants like Sisters of the New South and Randy's BBQ.

Chapter 6

PRODUCING LOWCOUNTRY PRODUCE

The concept of farm-to-table restaurants is not a modern fad. Long before corporate farming and genetically modified agricultural projects aimed at producing yields far beyond the soil and climate's natural capabilities, and even before massive restaurant chains led to a need for huge national conglomerate food distribution companies, "farm to table" is precisely how most local restaurants operated. Strangely, in just over sixty years since Ray Kroc convinced the McDonald brothers to streamline their operations and franchise their business nationwide, the concept of farm-to-table has come to be so different from the norm that it seems once again fresh and exciting. It may not be new, but organic farmers and farm-to-table restaurants in Savannah, and surely nationwide, are fighting a multifront war to bring this concept back to the American masses.

For many of these natural food soldiers, losing the war is not an option. For them, increasing the availability of fresh, organic produce is essential to the health of our children. They are adamant that removing chemicals and other unnatural agricultural products from the soil is crucial for the survival of our species. Moreover, the battle cry of these determined farmers, restaurateurs and advocates is that without responsible, organic and sustainable farming at the local level, our entire planet is at risk. There are certainly enough documentaries, books, articles and straightforward statistics that support this terrifying prospect.

But fighting massive corporate entities and their armies of lawyers and lobbyists to bring incredibly fresh produce and agricultural products developed solely from the dirt, climate and sweat of its workers doesn't have to be all about doom and gloom. It can be delicious. It can be exciting. It can be about tastes that truly represent locality. There is a growing movement in Savannah to prove exactly this point. Although this movement is mostly a recent development, it has been in the works for more than a decade. As more and more restaurants, farmers and specialty food shops join Savannah in this movement, the local food industry is finally getting back to its roots—literally.

Residents are taking up the cause, too. Groups like Savannah Urban Gardening Alliance (SUGA) work to help coordinate and assist residents with community gardening projects. The City of Savannah itself has worked to try to turn several empty lots across the city into community gardens with strict organic limitations. SUGA then helps to educate and aid residents in growing sustainable produce inside the city limits.

As SUGA and other similar groups continue to push residents to learn ways to grow and enjoy their own sustainable fruit and vegetables, and as other great restaurateurs pick up the cause, two men stand out as leading the charge in Savannah's restaurant scene to promote the quality of dining through organic, locally sourced produce: Michael Lacy of Cha Bella and Rafe and Ansley Rivers of Canewater Farm. Their stories help to illustrate what Savannah's food—grown within a short drive of the city—should taste like. What it used to taste like before the mega-corporatization of farming, before genetically modified vegetables and before harsh chemicals made it into our foods and irreparably altered their intended tastes.

Cha Bella Restaurant

The building itself seems organic. Michael Lacy, owner and chef of Cha Bella, agrees with that sentiment. Just about everything in the small, elegant East Broad Street restaurant is homemade and reclaimed. The fence across the south end of the stunning al fresco dining patio is from an old cargo ship container. There is an herb and small organic vegetable garden currently teeming with mint and sweet basil, which find their way into tasty dishes on the east side of the patio. The fine art paintings were donated by adoring (and extremely artistic) fans of Michael's cuisine. The enormous fork and knife art pieces bookending the original fireplace were made in-house from a collection of mismatched catering cutlery. When Michael was prepping the exterior wall of the patio for painting, he discovered the faint hint of one of the previous companies that owned the building and decided to try to carefully uncover as much of it as he could and restore it to some degree. This attention to detail and creativity in using otherwise discarded materials is at the center of everything for Michael Lacy. This goes doubly for his food.

There is no doubt that Michael was ahead of the curve. Nearly ten years before the likes of Mashama Bailey (The Grey), Hugh Acheson (The Florence) or Brandon Whitestone (Cotton & Rye) brought their respective versions of sprucing up local ingredients with their unique precision in the culinary arts, Michael Lacy brought the produce he grew on his own farm to the table of his own restaurant. Cha Bella began as a little restaurant to highlight the vegetables that Michael grew himself only a few miles away—a way to bring attention to the possibilities of urban organic farming. As Michael saw the demand grow for his seasonal and hyper-local cuisine, he passed the torch of his farm over to like-minded sustainable farmers—it is currently known as the Old Dairy Farm and provides organic dairy products to Savannah restaurants and specialty food shops like Smith Brothers Butcher Shop—so that he could focus on the restaurant. And what a restaurant it is.

The food at Cha Bella is exquisite. The objective of Michael's cooking is to let the local ingredients—and often hyper-local ingredients (those grown either on the premises itself or on the roof of Michael's nearby property)—shine through in each dish. Each plate is well thought out so that nothing overpowers the focus of the dish (often a local heirloom vegetable). The flavors are layered carefully, making each plate refined and sophisticated without being pretentious. For example, one of Michael's signature dishes is his Georgia White Shrimp and Risotto, which has won "Best Dish in Georgia" according to the Georgia Restaurant Association, Explore Georgia and Taste of Georgia. It's the creative chef's take on the Lowcountry classic shrimp and grits. Michael notes that his twist on the dish is more authentic to the area. Grits is a staple of most southern households, but it's made from corn, not often a product of the Lowcountry. On the other hand, rice became Savannah and the surrounding Lowcountry's first major cash crop. Michael's signature dish highlights two staple products of the Lowcountry without making it overly complicated. It is the chef's restraint that makes each bite of this sumptuous recipe so special.

In fact, Michael is so emphatic about showing off the quality of the ingredients that come into his restaurant that newly hired chefs often have a hard time adjusting. Cha Bella, for example, does not even have a freezer (other than the ice machines for beverages) on the premises. Similarly, the organic restaurant does not own a deep fryer, which Michael sees as not only a cheap and unsophisticated way of bringing crunch and saltiness to a dish but also a method of cooking that often destroys the nutrition and proper flavor of otherwise good ingredients. Such attention is spent on each ingredient that Michael challenges his entire kitchen staff to come up with ways to almost eliminate the need for trash cans. Every effort is made to use the entirety of each ingredient. Tail meat isn't discarded—it may turn into a carpaccio. The chef even goes so far as to demand that he receive his chickens and ducks whole from his farms to be sure that nothing is wasted. This way, he can turn liver into mousse, make stock and so on. The same goes for all of his ingredients that can't be used (e.g., husks, eggshells, stems and so on). They are not simply discarded but rather put aside to be collected by a local compost developer, allowing the nutrients to return to the soil to nourish the next crop.

By the end of the busy season, many of the newly hired chefs—who are often classically trained and recruited from top-tier Atlanta restaurants—are exhausted. Michael explained that many newly hired chefs don't make it on or don't want to make it on for another season because they know there is an easier way to do things. But easier is not better. This restaurateur goes to such extremes for each ingredient not just for the sake of the environment, the community or our well-being, but for the success of the restaurant as well. The thorough endeavors to waste nothing help Cha Bella keep its prices competitive. The point, after all, is to feed the community, not just the top 1 percent of the community.

While there may be a growing number of talented up-and-coming chefs in Savannah focusing on showcasing local, organic ingredients—Brandy Williamson of Local11Ten to mention one—there are few who promote sustainability quite as much as Michael Lacy. There is a lot of hope, but only time will tell whether future culinary history books will look back at this seasoned organic chef's heroic efforts as the beginning of Savannah's new culinary identity.

CANEWATER FARM AND THE CROPS THAT LOWCOUNTRY SOIL HAS PRODUCED

Rafe Rivers has an ancient and wise soul in spite of his relative youth. The wealth of knowledge and passion of this thirty-something farmer transcends any perceived lack of experience, having grown up playing on the streets of Atlanta rather than the marshes surrounding the Altamaha River. His intense sapphire gaze is the kind one can only get from having real life-changing experiences—the kind of experiences that take one from graduating from the University of Georgia to Uganda to work with aid organizations that assist local farmers. Those experiences left such an impact on Rafe that he went back to school at University of California–Santa Cruz to study agro-ecology and sustainable food systems. And yet in contrast to Rafe's intensity, his calm, warm demeanor almost suggests that his whole life has been spent on his fifty-acre farm just north of Darien, Georgia (what used to be the Scottish Highlanders' settlement, known then as New Inverness, and about one hour drive south of Savannah).

The farm is small, about fifty acres total, of which only about five to six acres are actually producing crops at any given time, while twenty

Rafe, owner of Canewater Farm, looking out over the marshes bordering his farm. 2016. *Donald Card.*

An oak lifting its mighty arms in praise on Canewater Farm. 2016. *Donald Card.*

acres remain naturally wooded; the other portions are rotated with cover crops so as not to overwork the soil. It is also impossibly beautiful. An enormous, ancient live oak explodes out of the earth a few hundred yards from the humble offices of Canewater Farm, commanding attention and respect. Rafe remarked that it is known as a "Praying Oak," as it has been throughout much of the history in this area. When he began to design the layout of the farm, which was mostly pine trees at the time, this Praying Oak became the center of the designs. No matter what else was contemplated, the Praying Oak would remain steadfast, overlooking the marshes and snaking creeks leading into the Altamaha River on one side and the easternmost fields of the farm on the other.

Growing organic vegetables in this sandy, mostly nutrient-deficient soil takes a lot of know-how. Even more so, it takes patience and a ton of hard work. To keep things truly local, Rafe and his team at Canewater refuse to bring in outside soil and never use any chemical-based fertilizer. Cover crops—mostly legumes such as cowpeas, clover and winter peas along with sudex, rye, sun hemp and oats (which have little resale value in grocery stores or restaurants)—are used to feed the soil in a process known as nitrogen fixation. The soil is then tested, and with luck, there is enough nitrogen and other nutrients to feed more valuable crops. After some research, conversing with other local organic farms and some experimentation, Rafe Rivers produced his first harvest of crops in 2013. The restaurant industry in Savannah was forever changed. It is no coincidence that Rafe Rivers's success developing elegant organic produce has paralleled the emergence of excellent farm-to-table Savannah restaurants like The Grey, Cotton & Rye and The Florence.

Canewater Farm, along with other notable organic operations, is bringing Savannah and the Lowcountry back to the actual tastes that come from the soil and climate of the land. Rafe Rivers is the guide into what ingredients would have been available to the residents of this area in the eighteenth and nineteenth centuries. We learned that as difficult as it was for the first European settlers of Savannah to produce crops in any sizable quantity save for the Salzburgers, with care, attention, some know-how, a caring community and a lot of hard work, the Lowcountry can produce amazing crops.

But as the record clearly shows (the failure of the Trustees' Garden), growing crops in Savannah and the surrounding area is supremely difficult. Rafe echoed the struggles of the original English settlers. The Lowcountry is intensely hot during the summer, making outdoor working conditions downright dangerous, not to mention stressful for plant life. The Lowcountry is also famous for its insects. Several species of insects and worms thrive on some of the freshly grown plants, but insects like biting gnats (also known as "noseeyums") and mosquitoes, so vicious during the cooler months, are more than just pests—they are also treacherous. In fact, mosquitoes caused one of the most disastrous epidemics in Savannah's history by spreading yellow fever across the city in 1876, killing more than 1,000 of its 28,000 residents in just two weeks. Having experienced two other outbreaks of yellow fever (1820 and 1854) that also collectively killed 1,700 people, when the 1876 outbreak occurred, those who could afford to flee did so, causing Savannah's population to shrink by another 5,000 residents.

If these conditions weren't challenging enough for farmers, it turns out that the soil itself is not necessarily ideal for wide varieties of crops. It is virtually sand, and almost nutrition-less sand. That is, unless one takes the time, energy and care to feed the soil. As Rafe paraphrased, "You have to feed the soil to feed the plants that feed you that will feed the community." Rafe carefully inspects composting companies and uses cover crops to feed his soil, which would likely have also been done by the original European farmers in the area in order to get any reasonable yields.

Prior to the chemicalization of fertilizer and use of toxic pesticides, these are exactly the conditions that the farmers who struggled to produce anything in the Trustees' Garden would have been contending with. As though to drive his point further, Rafe picked up a fistful of soil from the unnourished dirt road that surround his fields and then allowed the soil to sift through his fingers to his other hand. It was dry. It resembled sand from a child's dirty sandbox. Given all of these conditions, it is no wonder why English, Scottish and European Jewish settlers struggled to cultivate the land in the early years of settling Savannah.

Rafe knelt down next to one of his pepper plants, inspecting the rich red color of the Carmen peppers, which, unlike their green cousins, Padron and Shishitos, are actually best when they are red. The summer season of crops is coming to an end. The organic farmer smiled at the transition of the farm. The bright side of farming in the Lowcountry, he pointed out, is that if one were to overcome these woes—like the early Salzburgers did in the mid-1700s—one should be able to grow year-round. During the summer, Canewater will grow gumbo-worthy okra, fiery peppers, succulent eggplant and sweet potatoes, of which they also utilize the leaves (also known as sweet potato greens). During the winter,

Savannah restaurants and locals seek out Canewater fennel, arugula and winter greens.

While there is some evidence of those crops being grown here by the original European farmers of the late 1700s, the main ancient crops of those times were olives, rice and what is now known as Seminole pumpkins or Seminole squash.

In the new, yet-to-be-settled Americas, olives were of great interest to the Spanish explorers, like the famed Lucas Vasquez de Ayllon. Scholars now argue that this explorer set up his short-lived settlement, San Miguel de Gualdape, in 1526 around Sapelo Island, Georgia (about an hour's drive south of Savannah and across the marsh from Canewater Farm), rather than South Carolina, as previously thought. This settlement is the first ever European settlement in what is now the continental United States, preceding the English establishment of Jamestown by nearly 81 years. However, the settlement only lasted at most three months, as the two hundred settlers lost their leader, De Ayllon, shortly after the establishment of the small city. Nevertheless, it is believed that these Spaniards would have immediately begun olive production, as they had in California. Fast-forward 210 years and the English settlers who moved south from Savannah came across olive groves at what is now known as St. Simons Island (two hours' drive south of Savannah), and later, General Nathanael Greene discovered olive trees on his property in Cumberland Island, Georgia, where old Spanish missions once existed on what is now the Florida/Georgia border.

Georgia has since seen a resurgence of this ancient olive crop. Georgian farmers across the state are now producing olives for olive oils that are receiving worldwide recognition for their quality and taste. One such farm is the Terra Dolce Farm of Lyons, Georgia (seventy-two miles west of Savannah), which received a Gold Medal in 2014 at the New York International Olive Oil Competition. There were more than seven hundred olive oils from around the world that competed in that competition. Thus, although it may come as a surprise to many, olives and world-class olive oil production is a long-standing staple of the Savannah and Georgia diet.

Savannah and the Lowcountry are also rice communities. Rafe can point out a few locations within a short drive of Canewater Farm where the remnants of old rice paddies are still visible. The Scottish Highlanders may have had difficulty coming across rice in the 1730s and 1740s in the area (as was needed for their partan-bree, aka she-crab soup or crab stew).

By the 1750s, rice had become essential to the growth of the Georgia colony. However, rice is not native to the area. Originally, rice was brought over as part of the Columbian Exchange (an exchange of animals, plants and so on between America and Europe) to neighboring South Carolina by the early seventeenth century by the English, who were hoping to expand production in the Americas as had been done in Asia. By the 1750s, Georgia had begun to grow rice in areas south of Savannah, and soon rice would become Georgia's first staple crop. Unfortunately, the rice boom completed imploded after 130 years when commercial production in the United States moved west to Louisiana, Arkansas and even California. Rice production in Georgia went from its peak of 51 million pounds in 1859 to just over 8 million pounds in 1879 and eventually to only sixty thousand bushels (less than 2 million pounds) by 1919. As a result, the rice farming industry in Georgia was all but completely abandoned.

Indeed, the famed Revolutionary War hero Lachlan McIntosh earned a fortune in a rice plantation that he started only a few miles from where Rafe's farm is now, just off the Altamaha River. For fourteen years before he became heavily involved in the liberty efforts, McIntosh and one of his closest mentors from Charleston, the influential merchant Henry Laurens, partnered to make one of the most successful rice plantations that the Lowcountry ever saw. Given McIntosh's father's efforts in being the first commander of Savannah's guardians, as well as establishing New Inverness (now Darien, Georgia), not to mention Lachlan's success during the American Revolution, the county where his farm sat and the city his father established is known as McIntosh County. It also happens to be the same county where Rafe's Canewater Farm and other great organic farms like Walker Farms operate.

Another disappearing heirloom crop from the Lowcountry that Rafe points out is the Seminole pumpkin or Seminole squash. This small, pear-shaped pumpkin with a very hard rind was grown and utilized by several Creek nations, including the Miccosukees, and the Seminole nations of what is now Florida. It was a very important crop for those First Nations people, as it is a very hardy plant, capable of deterring insects, tolerating the heat and even evading mildew. It was known as the "hanging pumpkin" because many of the tribes would plant the seeds around the base of a trees to allow the vines to crawl up the tree. Among the various ways to enjoy this very distinctly flavored variety of pumpkin was Seminole pumpkin bread, which is still made for ceremonies by some of the Floridian tribes.

Unfortunately, however, gold was discovered in north Georgia in 1829 on Native American land, leading to the first big gold rush in the United States (a smaller gold rush in North Carolina occurred in 1799), and that initiated a chain of unfortunate events that would lead to one of America's darkest eras. Following the discovery of gold in north Georgia, a series of laws passed limiting what tribes could do on their own land. President Andrew Jackson shortly thereafter signed into law the Indian Removal Act of 1830 for the purpose of reclaiming land with valuable resources and to expand cotton plantations throughout Georgia and elsewhere. This, of course, is what eventually led to the Trail of Tears. As federal authorities removed the native people from their lands, they also removed their culture and heritage. There were many losses during this period. The most notable was the loss of life and liberty. Maybe the least recognized of these was the loss of many heirloom varieties of produce that were cultivated by the natives. These veggies were tilled and discarded, replaced by more profitable cash crops.

Rafe takes it upon himself, as do a growing number of farmers in the area, to reintroduce some incredible heirloom produce into the Lowcountry's diet. The steely-eyed farmer makes his rounds to farmers' markets and

Fields of veggies at Canewater Farm, with the greenhouse and barn sitting in the background. 2016. *Donald Card.*

restaurants, educating home cooks and top-tier restaurant chefs on the varieties of fruits and vegetables, many of which are completely foreign to buyers. Thankfully, Rafe's efforts have borne fruit. Most of Savannah's new crop of highly acclaimed restaurants—The Florence, The Grey, Cotton & Rye, Wyld, Green Truck Pub and Alligator Soul among them—are flocking to Canewater Farm for delicious Lowcountry soil–grown organic ingredients that will shape the next staple Savannah dish.

Rafe is quick to point out that he is not alone in McIntosh County, that there are farms that have been producing for years before him. Standing on the dock on the east side of the Canewater property, the young farmer stares out over the delta toward Sapelo Island, where Canewater is farming clams and oysters. Having spent several years just outside San Francisco, Rafe knows how much emphasis Marin County puts on its fresh, local and organic produce. There is still a long way to go, but Rafe can't help but beam at the idea that McIntosh County is on its way to become the agriculturally minded Marin County of the East. Granted, there is no Frank Lloyd Wright–designed Civic Center, as there is in the San Francisco Bay county to which Rafe compares his home county, but there is plenty of natural beauty and an accelerated interest and growth in the organic farming that is taking place here. Rafe may have a point when it comes to the natural beauty, as the Nature Conservancy has ranked the Altamaha River one of the seventy-five "Last Great Places" in the entire world. Bald eagles, woodpeckers, alligators and an almost uncountable number of other beautiful, rare wild species live virtually on Lachlan McIntosh's and Rafe River's back porch.

Whether they know it or not, Rafe and Ansley Rivers and other local farmers like them are at the center of Savannah's food renaissance, taking Savannah back to its roots, when the community was fed by the food that came from the plants grown in the soil of the community. There is simply no better way to know what Savannah food used to, is once again and should always taste like than enjoying deliciously prepared dishes using the heirloom crops coming out of Canewater Farm.

Chapter 7
SWEET ON HONEY

Harold MacMillan (British prime minister from 1957 to 1963) once famously said that "Britain's most useful role is somewhere between bee and dinosaur." The prime minister was referring at the time to the changing nature of Britain's role in the contemporary world—either being large and inefficient like a dinosaur or efficient but small and inconsequential like a bee. The philosophical prime minister's analogy that the bee lacks influence because it is small may have been a little misplaced. Much to the contrary, the honey bee has been argued to be the most important import for North American farming—ever.

But first things first. Honey bees are not indigenous to North America. Honey bees have not even been on the North American continent that long. Bees arrived in North America just three hundred years prior to Prime Minister MacMillan's famous quote, and it was the British who brought them. The first honey bees arrived from England in 1622 to what was then a very young Virginia colony. It didn't take long for the bees to spread throughout the colonies by way of swarms that could fly several miles at a time to set up new colonies of their own. In 1743, just ten short years after the founding of Savannah, Georgia had its first beehives. In less than one hundred years after that, bees were found as far west as Alaska. These first American bees were actually German bees, also known as the black bee. By 1860, America began importing Italian honey bees, which were known to be less defensive and generally stock excessive amounts of honey—far more than the bees need for themselves.

Savannah's bustling Broughton Street in the early 1900s (note the Bee Hive sign). Circa 1915. *Detroit Publishing Company, Publisher.*

Almost immediately upon seeing bees in the 1740s, Savannah recognized the utilitarian nature of these creatures—so much so, in fact, that the state has identified at least fifty crops aided by bee pollination that may not exist otherwise. As a result, the honey bee is honored as the state insect of Georgia.

The long, proud history of beekeeping in the Peach State is evident by the fact that some of the United States' most esteemed beekeepers have come from Georgia. One such beekeeper was Georgia-raised Sarah Elizabeth Sherman, who moved to Texas after the Civil War and became Texas's most successful commercial beekeeper. But it was the "Georgia Bee King" (also known as the "Dixie Beekeeper"), J.J. Wilder, who put Georgia beekeeping on the map. The Georgia Bee King was one of the most successful and largest beekeepers in the entire country. At his pinnacle, Wilder managed more than fifteen thousand hives across the East Coast through various partnerships. As the head of the Georgia Beekeepers Association, as well as with his book, *Wilder's System of Beekeeping*, along with regular articles in his *Dixie Bee Journal*, Wilder spread his beekeeping techniques and knowledge throughout the United States. This became particularly helpful during World War I and World War II, when sugar supply in the country was drastically cut. Honey production ramped up to compensate. Honey became the staple sweetener in a country that didn't originally have honey bees until 1947, when sugar could finally be purchased again without the use of rationing stamps.

Beyond being a sweetener, honey has been one of the most important commodities in history, and not just in Georgia. Due to honey's antifungal, antimicrobial, antibacterial nature, it has been used as a natural remedy for a whole host of ailments. Burn victim wards of hospitals still use honey today to treat wounds, and veterinarians also use honey to treat many animal injuries, including injuries to wild and endangered animals. One doesn't have to look back very far to see evidence of honey being the prime medicine used in the United States up until World War II, when chemical companies began pushing pharmaceuticals.

Although the days of rationing sugar have long past, the need for beekeeping education is at an all-time high. A great effort has been put into educating the masses about the importance of bees on our agriculture and our livelihood in recent years, due to a number of factors such as bee population loss and the overarching whole foods movement. Fittingly, at the center of the world's discussion about the importance of beekeeping—with projects like the "Bee Cause"—is another Lowcountry beekeeper: Savannah Bee Company's Ted Dennard.

SAVANNAH BEE COMPANY

Almost certainly, most landowners would have turned down Old Roy Hightower's odd request. The thought of having thousands of bees as tenants on your property is enough to put anyone off. Thankfully, Tom Dennard had played golf with the old beekeeper and was intrigued by his vision. Hightower had his eye on the tupelo trees on Dennard's property in Brunswick known as Hostel in the Forest (about one and a half hours' drive south of Savannah), from which his bees could gather that most coveted nectar. Instead of turning the beekeeper away, Tom proposed a deal: Old Roy could leave his hives on Dennard's property, but only if he would teach his young, impressionable surfing son, Ted, everything he knew about beekeeping. So begins the legend of the beekeeper Ted Dennard and his Savannah Bee Company.

With the terms agreed on, Old Roy began his lessons by warning Ted that beekeeping will "become a way of life." These words proved all too

Ted Dennard, owner and head beekeeper of Savannah Bee Company, managing hives with a mask on. *Savannah Bee Company.*

true, as Ted became passionate about the entire process of keeping bees and harvesting honey. Ted began his own hives and kept bees all through high school. And then through college. And then went on to the Peace Corps, where he ended up teaching beekeeping to villages in Jamaica.

In fact, when Ted returned to his beloved Lowcountry, he continued to keep bees in his small apartment on Jones Street in downtown Savannah. It should be noted that until recently, keeping bees downtown was illegal. Nevertheless, Ted found room in his bathtub for the hives as he worked on spreading beekeeping on the Oatland Island Wildlife Center, just a few miles east of downtown. As the hives produced an abundance of honey—far more than the bees actually needed—Ted sought out emptied wine bottles from his friends to store the golden surplus. He would bottle a few hundred milliliters for himself but didn't quite know what to do with any remaining bottles. A close friend and owner of a small boutique shop, One Fish Two Fish, a few blocks from Ted's house, agreed to sell them in her shop.

Ted didn't stop with simply bottling the honey. As he had learned from the very beginning, there was so much more to beekeeping than producing honey. The budding entrepreneur didn't waste any product of the bee. Wax and essential oils were combined to make lip balms and body products. Other products, like candles, were also in the works shortly thereafter.

Even in this early segment of the Ted's business, Ted set out to create distinct monofloral honeys. He knew that honeys will take on varying degrees of sweetness, flavor and floral aromas depending on which flowers the bees received their nectar from. But to make a true monofloral honey, Ted would need to find locations where there was only one nectar source in a three-mile radius of the hive. If the bees were to go to any other nectar source, the honeycomb would be a mix of different-flavored honeys. However, knowing that bees practice flower fidelity—an ultra-efficient system of collecting the entire nectar from one location until it is completely depleted—Ted had a chance of collecting some pretty spectacular honeys.

With this in mind, Ted set out to find locations along the Altamaha River and Okefenokee Swamp (near the Florida/Georgia line) where he might be able to produce tupelo honey. This would be no easy feat. Monofloral honeys are not only more difficult to obtain than wildflower, given the amount of planning that is required, but tupelo itself also involves often perplexing logistics and immeasurable amounts of luck. First, the tupelo is a swamp-based tree; in fact, the name is an Anglicization of the Creek tribes' word for swamp tree. This means that getting the beehives out to where they are in range of the tupelo tree can be extremely challenging. Ted and company describe at times having to float the hives down the river on barges. Assuming one has found an area where there are only the flowers of the tupelo blossoming at that time (so a true monofloral can be accomplished), there is the still the tupelo flower itself to contend with. There are reports of the flower being in bloom for just a few days out of the year. However, if one is successful in producing a monofloral tupelo honey, as Ted was and continues to be, one would have one of the most highly regarded and most sought-after honeys in the world.

The desirability of the tupelo honey is multifaceted. The flavor itself is highly desired due to its light, non-overpowering taste, making it a popular honey among tea drinkers and those using honey as a sugar substitute. The sugar makeup of the honey also adds to its appeal. Tupelo honey sugar makeup is almost exclusively fructose, with only trace amounts of glucose. Glucose has a much lower solubility in water, which causes it to crystalize rather quickly. On the other hand, fructose is comfortable in a more liquid state, meaning that honeys with high fructose levels and low glucose levels, like tupelo honey, will take a very, very long time to crystalize. To wit, it is said that the three-thousand-year-old honey found in King Tut's tomb was not only still edible but also *not yet* fully crystalized. It should be noted that crystallization of honey does not denote its edibility but merely its taste and texture. Honey is one of the only truly non-perishable foods. And tupelo honey has come to be known as the gold standard of honey for all of these properties.

Demand grew for Ted's tupelo honey. It didn't take long before he needed to move production out of his kitchen. By 1998, despite still working a full-time job, Ted had developed a fast-growing wholesale operation with other high-end specialty boutiques like Dean & DeLuca, putting Ted's honey on their shelves. By 2002, Ted had left his job and finally, formally started Savannah Bee Company as he moved his production to an eight-hundred-square-foot classroom on Wilmington Island (part of unincorporated Savannah, twelve miles from Historic Downtown Savannah). Following a Fancy Food Show early the next year, where Ted excitedly displayed his products, orders began flooding in from Neiman Marcus, Williams-Sonoma and Crate & Barrel, causing Ted to once again consider expanding. Savannah Bee Company's warehouse on Wilmington Island is now more than forty thousand square feet.

The incredible success in the wholesale business gave Savannah's favorite beekeeper the opportunity to do something close to his heart: educate. In 2008, Ted opened up the first Savannah Bee Company retail shop on Broughton Street. Ted knew that success of a retail shop centered on honey- and beeswax-related products would be a long shot—even outright risky. Nevertheless, Ted felt it was important to have a place where he could educate the public on bees, the benefits of honey and immense variety of natural, useful and delicious products that come from bees. But while the focus may have initially been to educate and inform the public about honey, the store was, in fact, a huge commercial success, requiring once again that Savannah Bee Company expand to now five separate retail shops. These successes have led to write-ups in places like *Inc. Magazine* and news segments on CNN.

So much attention has been given to Ted Dennard's success and the influence on beekeeping in Georgia, the United States and even the world that it often goes unnoticed how the Savannah Bee Company has affected the culinary scene in Savannah. Most Savannahians know that there is no better complement to strong, rich cheeses—such as Aztec cheddar or Dragon's Breath from Flat Creek Lodge Dairy Farm of Swainsboro, Georgia—like raw honeycomb. Just like many households in Savannah, many restaurants such as Olde Pink House and Local11Ten serve their cheese platters with Savannah Bee Company honeycomb. Restaurants are also using local Georgia honey (often tupelo and sourwood) in glazes for fish, seafood and pork, as well as making barbecue sauces and marinades out of the sticky sweetness. One would be hard-pressed to find a good restaurant in Savannah that doesn't utilize local honey. Thanks to Georgia's rich beekeeping history and people like Ted Dennard, honey is undoubtedly one of Savannah's most prized ingredients.

Chapter 8
IN THE MIDST OF A FOOD RENAISSANCE

It's an awareness of what this city has to offer the culinary world. It's an excitement around the restaurants and the food that the chefs are bringing to the table. It's accepting and embracing the entirety of the city's past. It's trusting that the next generation of aspiring and inspiring cooks will respect Savannah's rich history while not being afraid to break new ground. It's continuing to enjoy a creamy crab stew at longtime Savannah favorites like Crystal Beer Parlor and 17Hundred90 Inn. It's giving new hit dishes like Dirty Duck Rice at The Grey a chance to become a new Savannah signature dish. Savannah's restaurant renaissance has just begun, and with an average of more than 13 million visitors to the Hostess City every year, the word will spread like pecan butter over fresh-baked biscuits.

Savannah is starting to team with hot new restaurants eager to show their brand of locally inspired next-generation dishes. To give some perspective of how new this restaurant renaissance is, consider that prior to 2008 there were really only two fine dining establishments to speak of in the city: Elizabeth on 37th and the Sapphire Grill. The oldest of those two restaurants is the always elegant Elizabeth on 37th, which has firmly established itself as the premier restaurant in the city since 1981. Chef and owner Elizabeth Terry originally ran the kitchen showcasing Lowcountry coastal seafood and fresh produce. Current executive chef Kelly Yambor is proudly and successfully maintaining the impeccable cuisine for which the restaurant has been known for thirty-five years.

In 1998, Chef Christopher Nolan—who just two years earlier had been recognized in the *New York Times* for his culinary skills for restaurants he headed in Charleston—opened the fresh-market concept restaurant of Sapphire Grill. The Pennsylvania-born Nolan perfected his southern palate in Charleston for eight years before taking on Savannah and has received glowing reviews ever since. Awarded by the Distinguished Restaurants of North America (DiRONA), Sapphire Grill's menu changes constantly to highlight only the best ingredients that the fresh-market team can source from season to season. While many first-time visitors to the city may line up for a buffet at Paula Deen's Lady and Sons directly next door, Sapphire Grill has stood as a strong example of Savannah's fine dining cuisine for twenty years for patrons looking for something a little more refined.

But it is really only in the last eight years or so that Savannah has seen great growth in not just fine dining but in world-class cuisine in general. At the forefront of this movement is Local11Ten, which has been one of Savannah's most successful fine dining establishments since at least 2009, when General Manager Jamie Durrence took the helm. Classically trained at Le Cordon Bleu in Orlando, Executive Chef Brandy Williamson has certainly put her stamp on Savannah's cuisine with recognition in the *New York Times*, awards by DiRONA and commendations by Best Chefs America. Pairing breathtaking food with some of the world's best wine has also led to the restaurant receiving the Award of Excellence from *Wine Spectator* magazine.

In 2014, Savannah began to see an explosion of world-class chefs just starting to discover Savannah. Chef superstar Hugh Acheson—James Beard Award recipient and someone recognized as the Best New Chef by *Food & Wine* magazine—put a southern spin on central Italian dishes in opening The Florence. It is genuinely and pleasingly surprising to see how much it makes sense to integrate southern cooking techniques and local ingredients into otherwise Italian dishes. Shortly after the opening of The Florence, Chef Mashama Bailey—who earned her cooking chops working alongside Bib-Gourmand recipient Gabrielle Hamilton of Manhattan's Prune—opened The Grey, a shockingly beautiful and creative restaurant in the ruins of Savannah's old Greyhound terminal, with an enormous amount of fanfare. Added to this list of who's-who of noteworthy chefs who have graced Savannah's dining scene over the past few years is Cotton & Rye's Chef Brian Whitestone, who trained under another James Beard Award recipient and farm-to-table pioneer, Allen Susser. This exquisite but casual southside restaurant is simple, locally sourced (think Canewater Farm) and flatly outstanding.

Beyond the restaurants with big-name chefs in the kitchen, there is a large number of creative restaurants serving outstanding food from lesser-known but no less talented chefs. The Ordinary Pub, Treylor Park and Hitch are spoiling Savannahians with delectable new signature dishes. The Ordinary Pub's classically trained chef Zach Starr is wowing locals with dishes like Kentucky Bourbon Barrel Ale Braised Pork Belly and Ousso Buca Chicken Chops. Similarly, Trey Wilder's fun and funky restaurants of Treylor Park and Hitch are serving up sinfully delicious bites like Duck Pot Pie Egg Rolls and PB&J Wings (pecan butter wings with a peach jam sauce).

Further proof of the Hostess City's booming restaurant renaissance is seen in the number of beautiful international restaurants setting roots here. For example, without buying a transatlantic airline ticket, residents and visitors just can't get closer to feeling as though they were in a Paris bistro than dining at Circa 1875 on Whitaker Street; the ambiance and attention to detail in the modern French restaurant and menu are mesmerizing. But there really hasn't been a more successful restaurant family in Savannah than husband-and-wife team Ele and Sean Tran, who at last count had six consistently busy and well-reviewed restaurants in Savannah and at least one in Charleston. Ele's story from escaping Vietnam as a toddler with her family following the Siege of Saigon to becoming one of the most influential restaurateurs in Savannah is inspiring. Yet it is the staggering variety of incredibly delicious Asian-inspired restaurants—from Fire Street Food to Flying Monk Noodle Bar, Chive Sea Bar & Lounge and the new and fun restaurant, The Vault—that really have the locals in awe.

There is also evidence that this renaissance has just begun. Well-established and highly regarded restaurants in other places are giving the city a shot. Savannah has already received one great Charleston-based restaurant (Rue De Jean) recently and is anxiously awaiting the arrival of one of Charleston's most awarded restaurants, Sean Brock's Husk, in 2017. Brock, having received multiple James Beard Awards (Rising Star, Outstanding Chef and Best Chef: Southeast), as well as having garnered *Bon Appétit*'s Best Restaurant in America commendation, may be one of the most decorated chefs to open a restaurant in Savannah ever. Nevertheless, with now at least a half dozen kitchens in this small city being overseen by women and men having earned their stripes under some of the world's most respected chefs, it is only moments away that the names of Savannah's chefs will be household names the world over.

There is no doubt that this beautifully framed and quirky city of saints and sinners is entering its prime on the world's dining stage. And although this journey began with the two of us trying to get to the heart of Savannah's food history and culinary identity, we are blissfully satisfied with the idea that as tasty as the city's past is, the best plates have yet to be served.

BIBLIOGRAPHY

To learn more about Savannah's restaurants, specialty food shops and personalities mentioned in this book or to begin planning your next trip to the beautifully delicious Savannah, Georgia, please visit SavannahTasteExperience.com and consider the following list of websites.

WEBSITES

Boar's Head Grill & Tavern. http://boarsheadgrillandtavern.com.
Byrd's Famous Cookies. http://www.byrdcookiecompany.com.
Canewater Farm. http://www.canewaterfarm.com.
Cha Bella. http://www.cha-bella.com.
Charlie J. Russ's Seafood. http://www.russoseafood.com.
Cotton & Rye. http://www.cottonandrye.com.
The Crystal Beer Parlor. http://www.crystalbeerparlor.com.
The Florence. http://www.theflorencesavannah.com.
The Grey. http://thegreyrestaurant.com.
Local11Ten. http://www.local11ten.com.
Molly MacPherson's Scottish Pub. https://macphersonspub.com.
The Ordinary Pub. http://www.theordinarypub.com/#home.
Pie Society. http://thebritishpiecompany.com.
Sapphire Grill. http://www.sapphiregrill.com.
Savannah Bee Company. http://savannahbee.com.

Savannah Taste Experience Food Tours. https://www.savannahtasteexperience.com.

17Hundred90 Inn & Restaurant. http://17hundred90.com.

Smith Brothers Butcher Shop. http://www.smithbrothersbutchershop.com.

Tondee's Tavern. http://www.tondees.com.

Treylor Park/Hitch. http://www.treylorpark.com.

Walls' BBQ. https://www.facebook.com/search/327519797420850/local_search?surface=tyah.

Zunzi's TakeOut and Catering. http://zunzis.com.

Interviews

Anderson, Brenda. In-person interview, July 7, 2016.

Anderson, Robert. In-person interview, July 7, 2016.

Gottlieb, Michael. In-person interview, July 28, 2016.

Griffin, Gary. In-person interview, July 7, 2016.

Lacy, Michael. In-person interview, August 24, 2016.

Nichols, John. In-person interview, July 20, 2016.

Rivers, Rafe. In-person interview, August 23, 2016.

Russo, Charlie, Jr. In-person interview, July 19, 2016.

Weston, Teresa. In-person interview, August 10, 2016.

Books

Aldrich, April. *A History of Honey in Georgia and the Carolinas*. Charleston, SC: The History Press, 2015.

Berendt, John. *Midnight in the Garden of Good and Evil*. New York: Vintage Books, 1994.

Gottlieb, Isser. *Gottlieb's Bakery: Savannah's Sweetest Tradition*. Charleston, SC: The History Press, 2011.

Hudson, Charles M., and Carmen Chaves Tesser. *Forgotten Centuries: Indians and Europeans in the American South, 1521–1704*. Athens: University of Georgia Press, 1994.

ONLINE SOURCES

Anson Mills. "Savannah Red Rice." http://www.ansonmills.com/recipes/403.

Area Connect. "Savannah City, Georgia Statistics and Demographics." http://savannah.areaconnect.com/statistics.htm.

Banks, Jessica. "All Bread Is Not Created Equal." Medieval Technology and American History: In Depth Articles. http://www.engr.psu.edu/mtah/articles/all_bread_not_equal.htm.

The Bee Queen. "Why Honey Crystallizes." https://www.bee-queen.com/why-honey-crystallizes.

Binder, Laura. "Red Rice: The South's Classiest Classic." *Savannah Now*, February 2007. http://savannahnow.com/accent/2007-02-20/red-rice-souths-classiest-classic.

Biography. "Clarence Thomas Biography." http://www.biography.com/people/clarence-thomas-9505658.

Blake, John. "Three Questions for Clarence Thomas." CNN, June 25, 2013. http://www.cnn.com/2013/06/09/us/clarence-thomas-three-questions.

Brooks, Ron. "Georgia's Ogeechee River American Shad Run." About Sports. http://saltfishing.about.com/od/americanandhickoryshad/a/aa070109a.htm.

The Bureau of Labor Statistics. "CPI Inflation Calculator." http://www.bls.gov/data/inflation_calculator.htm.

Burton, Neel, MD. "The Meaning of Nostalgia." *Psychology Today*, November 26, 2014. https://www.psychologytoday.com/blog/hide-and-seek/201411/the-meaning-nostalgia.

Butler, Ty. "Don't Miss Out on Georgia's Shad Run." *Savannah Now*, February 11, 2010. http://savannahnow.com/sports/2010-02-11/dont-miss-out-georgias-shad-run.

Charleston County Public Library. "Transatlantic Linkage: The Gullah/Geechee-Sierra Leone Connection." From an exhibit brochure presented by the Museum of Coastal History and the Sierra Leone National Museum. Used here courtesy of the Coastal Georgia Historical Society. http://www.ccpl.org/content.asp?id=15719&catID=6042&action=detail&parentID=5748.

CLR search.com. "Savannah Populations by Race and Ethnicity." http://www.clrsearch.com/Savannah-Demographics/GA/Population-by-Race-and-Ethnicity.

Coclanis, Peter A. "Rice." New Georgia Encyclopedia. http://www. georgiaencyclopedia.org/articles/business-economy/rice.

Coon, Dean. "Time Travel: The Liberty Boys were Savannah's Revolutionaries." *Savannah Now,* July 18, 2014. http://savannahnow.com/ column-accent/2014-07-18/time-travel-liberty-boys-were-savannahs-revolutionaries.

The Crystal Beer Parlor. "The Legend Lives On: The History of Crystal Beer Parlor." http://www.crystalbeerparlor.com/history.php.

Daniels, Greg C. "Sapelo Island Shell Rings." Lost Worlds, February 24, 2012. http://lostworlds.org/sapelo_shell_rings.

Dawers, Bill. "City Talk: Crystal Beer Parlor Turns 80." BIS, December 22, 2013. http://businessinsavannah.com/bis/2013-12-22/city-talk-crystal-beer-parlor-turns-80.

Deane, Green. "Seminole Pumpkins." Eat the Weeds and Other Things Too. http://www.eattheweeds.com/cucurbita-muschata-seminole-edible-2.

Duplain, Becky. "Destruction of Native American Culture." Angels & Ghosts. http://www.angelsghosts.com/destruction-of-native-american-culture.

Fogleman, Aaron Spencer. "Moravians." New Georgia Encyclopedia. http://www.georgiaencyclopedia.org/articles/arts-culture/moravians.

Gatlin, Tasha. "Burgers, Beer and Good Times: Memories Clash with Reality of Closing Crystal Beer Parlor." *Savannah Now*, December 29, 2000. http://savannahnow.com/stories/122900/LOCcrystalmemories. shtml#.V5avyVeCzzI.

Geering, Deborah. "At Least This Compromise Comes with Peaches." *Atlanta Magazine*, May 22, 2013. http://www.atlantamagazine.com/ dining-news/at-least-this-compromise-comes-with-peaches.

Georgia Historical Society. "Struggles of the Late 19th Century." http:// georgiahistory.com/education-outreach/online-exhibits/online-exhibits/three-centuries-of-georgia-history/nineteenth-century/ struggles-of-the-late-19th-century.

The Georgia Museum & Hall of Fame. "2011 Career Achievement Inductee Burl Womack." http://www.grhof.com/2011%20CA%20Burl%20 Womack.htm.

Georgia Olive Growers Association. "Terra Dolce of Lyons, GA Wins Gold Medal at New York International Olive Oil Competition." April 18, 2014. http://georgiaolivegrowers.com/terra-dolce-lyons-ga-wins-gold-metal-new-york-international-olive-oil-competition.

Georgia Sport Fishing Regulations. "Shrimp, Crab, Shellfish & Bait Minnows." http://www.eregulations.com/georgia/fishing/shrimp-crab-shellfish-bait-minnows.

The Great British Meat Co. "Butcher's Guide to the British Banger." http://greatbritishmeat.com/recipes-and-tips/miscellany/butchers-sausage-history.html.

Harrison, Don. "ASMFC American Shad Sustainable Fishing Plan for Georgia." Georgia Department of Natural Resources. http://www.asmfc.org/files/Shad%20SFMPs/gaShadSFMP.pdf.

Historical Insights. "Russian Immigration to America 1880–1910." http://www.ancestry.com/historicalinsights/russian-immigration-1800s.

Johnson, Ben. "Haggis, Scotland's National Dish." Historic UK. http://www.historic-uk.com/HistoryUK/HistoryofScotland/Haggis-Scotlands-National-dish.

Kennedy, Iain. "The Flyting of Dunbar and Kennedy." Kennedy One—Name Study. http://www.kennedydna.com/flyting_of_dunbar_and_kennedy.htm.

Krewer, Gerard. "History of Olive Growing in Georgia." Georgia Olive Growers Association. http://georgiaolivegrowers.com/resources-research/history.

Lagiminoiere, Alyssa. "Sorry Charlie's Campaign." http://alyssalagimoniere.com/assets/pdfs/sorry_char_book.pdf.

Larson, Scott. "Owner, Tenant at Odds about Sorry Charlie's." *Savannah Now*, June 20, 2007. http://savannahnow.com/news/2007-06-20/owner-tenant-odds-about-sorry-charlies.

The Local Palate. "Gottlieb's Bakery Returns to Savannah." http://thelocalpalate.com/articles/gottliebs-bakery-returns-to-savannah.

Megathlin, Carol. "Book Tells Clary's Story." *Savannah Now*, March 20, 2009. http://savannahnow.com/accent/2009-03-20/book-tells-clarys-story.

Moss, Robert F. "Roe Is Me: One Man's She-Crab Odyssey through the Streets of Charleston." *Charleston City Paper*, July 30, 2008. http://www.charlestoncitypaper.com/charleston/roe-is-me/Content?oid=1115367.

Online Etymology Dictionary. "Grits." http://www.etymonline.com/index.php?term=grits.

Our Georgia History. "Clarence Thomas." http://www.ourgeorgiahistory.com/ogh/clarence_thomas.

Peltz, James F. "Outdoor Grill Industry Tries to Keep Sales Sizzling." *Los Angels Times*, July 4, 2016. http://www.latimes.com/business/la-fi-agenda-outdoor-grills-20160704-snap-story.html.

Pop, Larisa. "Salzburg's History: Coming a Long Way." Scribd. https://www.scribd.com/document/231546725/Salzburg.

Powers Stramm, Polly. "Old Fort Neighborhood Rekindles Warm Memories." *Savannah Now*, November 26, 2001. http://savannahnow.com/stories/112601/LOCpolly.shtml#.V7DlpVeqS-I.

Rabeler, Julianna. "The Savannah Bee Company: Part One, In the Beginning." Savannah Bee Company, April 19, 2016. http://savannahbee.com/blog/the-savannah-bee-company-part-one-in-the-beginning.

———. "The Savannah Bee Company: Part Three, Hope and a Promise." Savannah Bee Company, August 11, 2016. http://savannahbee.com/blog/savannah-bee-company-part-iii-hope-and-a-promise.

———. "The Savannah Bee Company: Part Two, It's Been a Wild Ride." Savannah Bee Company, May 23, 2016. http://savannahbee.com/blog/savannah-bee-company-part-two-its-been-a-wild-ride.

Rawlins, Elizabeth. "Sorry Charlie's Receives Facelift." World Now, August 19, 2014. http://apmobile.worldnow.com/story/26319953/sorry-charlies-receives-facelift.

Recipes from a German Grandma. "History of Bratwurst." http://www.kitchenproject.com/german/Bratwurst/history.htm.

Red Orbit. "American Shad." http://www.redorbit.com/reference/american_shad.

Rodbard, Matt. "9 Things to Know About Gullah Geechee Cuisine." Zagat, February 29, 2016. https://www.zagat.com/b/9-things-to-know-about-gullah-geechee-cuisine.

Sankowski, Andrew. "Barbacoa: The Origin of Barbecue." American Studies 2001: Introduction to American Studies. http://amst2001.neatline-uva.org/neatline/show/barbecue#records/947.

Sausage Wiki. "Blood Sausage." http://sausage.wikia.com/wiki/Blood_sausage.

Savannah Bee Company. "Savannah Bee Company Overview." http://savannahbee.com/media/SBC_2014PressKit.pdf.

Savannah Community Gardens. http://www.savannahga.gov/DocumentCenter/View/3116.

Savannah for 91 Days. "Johnson Square." http://savannah.for91days.com/johnson-square.

Savannah Now. "The Big One that (Almost) Got Away: High Winds Blow Down Neon Fish Sign, a City Market Fixture for Nearly 60 Years." January 18, 2006. http://savannahnow.com/stories/011806/3582638.shtml#.V5Z71VeCzzJ.

————. "Isser Gottlieb." Obituaries. http://www.legacy.com/obituaries/savannah/obituary.aspx?pid=161963514.

Shaw, Hank. "American Shad: Eating and Cooking Tips." About Food. http://fishcooking.about.com/od/meetyourfish/p/shad_profile.htm.

Slow Food USA. "Ark of Taste: Seminole Pumpkins." https://www.slowfoodusa.org/ark-item/seminole-pumpkin.

South Carolina: Just Right. "A History of Gullah Cuisine." http://discoversouthcarolina.com/articles/how-rice-built-a-lowcountry-legacy.

Sumpter, Althea. "Geechee and Gullah Culture." New Georgia Encyclopedia, March 11, 2016. http://www.georgiaencyclopedia.org/articles/arts-culture/geechee-and-gullah-culture.

The United States Census Bureau. "The Black Population: 2010." http://www.census.gov/prod/cen2010/briefs/c2010br-06.pdf.

————. "QuickFacts: Savannah City, Georgia." http://www.census.gov/quickfacts/chart/PST045214/1369000.

Visit Historic Savannah. "Historic Johnson Square." http://www.visit-historic-savannah.com/johnsonsquare.html.

Wojciechowski, Martin F., and Johanna Mahn. "Nitrogen Fixation and the Nitrogen Cycle." Tree of Life Web Project. http://tolweb.org/notes/?note_id=3920.

INDEX

ABOUT THE AUTHORS

Brothers Stu and Donald Card—Stu a partner of a busy law firm and Donald a broadcast operations specialist for a major news outlet—fell in love with Savannah and its food culture when they came to a career crossroads. With the long, rich history, beautiful architecture, amazing people and unique Lowcountry speed of life, it didn't take them long to realize that their future laid in showing off the Hostess City's greatest bites. Out of this passion grew the highly rated, award-winning food tour, Savannah Taste Experience. Stu and Donald's research, operations and development of historical stories for Savannah Taste Experience has entertained tens of thousands of guests for more than five years now. It is this perspective running deliciously fun food tours in the Historic District that led the brothers to put some of these fascinating stories on paper. This is Stu and Donald's first published book.